Legal Immigrant, Illegal Immigrant

✦

What Made This Country Great and What Will Tear It Apart

Franco Ferrari

iUniverse, Inc.
New York   Bloomington

Legal Immigrant, Illegal Immigrant

What Made This Country Great
and What Will Tear It Apart

iUniverse books may be ordered through booksellers or by contacting:

iUniverse
1663 Liberty Drive
Bloomington, IN 47403
www.iuniverse.com
1-800-Authors (1-800-288-4677)

ISBN: 978-1-4401-0261-5 (pbk)
ISBN: 978-1-4401-0262-2 (ebk)

Printed in the United States of America

Dedication

For Patricia, my wife "First Time I Ever Saw Your Face."
Luigi and Clarissa - my pride of fatherhood.
My parents and family for their sacrifice in providing a better
life.
All the legal immigrants who take pride in America.
All the American soldiers who protect the rights of others
worldwide.
All the generous Americans who give unselfishly and are always
there for those in need.
To my Brother Knights of Columbus for their undying love of
God, family and country.
Also thanks to my editor Jeremy Lazar, who would like to thank
his parents, his brother Marc, Jay Jay, Lauren and Mike for
all their help and support, and of course - This one's for you
Grandpa!

Thank You.

"In the first place we should insist that if the immigrant who comes here in good faith becomes an American and assimilates himself to us. He shall be treated on an exact equality with everyone else for it is an outrage to discriminate against any such men because of creed or birthplace or origin but this is predicated upon the persons becoming in every facet an American, and nothing but an American. There can be no divided allegiance here. Any man who says he is an American but something else also is not American at all. We have room for but one flag - the American flag. We have room for but one language here, and that is the English language and we have room for one soul loyalty and that is loyalty to the American people."

- Theodore Roosevelt, 1907

Introduction

Why am I writing this book? For that matter, why should you care that I'm writing this book? Do you love America? I do. I always have, even though I was born in Italy.

Today I'm proud that I can call myself an American. I'm proud that today I'm a successful multi-business owner, but it wasn't always that way. Italy was devastated after World War II, and my family had to struggle to put food on the table. We dreamt of coming to America - the Land of Opportunity.

And we arrived, but not without struggle and sacrifice

However, this book is not just about me, nor is it just my story. My story is almost inconsequential. I'm only one of millions and millions of immigrants who have come to this country. We all have a similar story to share. We all have the same love for America.

We have all seen the greatness and have received the goodness. This country has helped us grow and prosper. Once hitting these shores, we worked hard not only for ourselves, or for our families, but for the country as a whole.

I'm writing this book because I love America. Often times - especially in the last few years - it seems that people are forgetting what a wonderful country America is, and how much we have given to the world. My story is merely a vehicle for you to reflect on all of the wonderful things that this country gives to its citizens and others around the world.

I'm writing this book because I want to get the message across that this country is the best in the world and that the system works when people have respect for the laws. I want you to see America through the eyes of an immigrant. A *legal* immigrant.

Because I'm a legal immigrant, and because my family and I had to fight so hard to get here, I've never taken anything that this country has given me for granted. Because I'm a legal immigrant I understand what a danger illegal immigration is to this country that I love.

There are two ways to become an American: You can come to America the right way and be both a legal immigrant and be a good, productive, law abiding citizen; or you can break the law, usurping the system at the expense of law abiding citizens. You can sneak across the border and live your life as an illegal alien.

That's right, you won't find any political correctness in this book. Let's call it like it is - Those who slip into this country are not illegal immigrants, but illegal aliens.

We must guard against those who want to sneak in without obeying the laws, who want to take from our bounty without giving back and without earning the right. If we let them, these illegal aliens will tear down this country.

I want to show Americans what a truly incredible country they live in from an immigrant's perspective. I think that a native citizen would appreciate the benefits of the United States even more if they saw it through the eyes of someone who wasn't born here.

These differences are more noticeable to immigrants, because they can compare their life after arriving in America to their life before. A natural born American may be grateful for what this country offers, but may not really appreciate it to the depth of one who had to live without all those benefits for many years, and is now very thankful for having all of the wonderful things that are here in the United States.

I'm writing this book because I want to get the message across that America really is the best country in the world, and I hope you care because I, for one, would like to keep it that way.

PART I

Why I Loved America
Before I Ever Set Foot
Upon Her Shores

Chapter 1

This may be my life story, but the story doesn't start with me. In the early part of the twentieth century immigrants came in droves to the United States, including both of my grandfathers. It was a hard journey, and once arriving in America, many immigrants weren't allowed in.

Once the lucky ones set foot on American soil, they still had to find a way to make a living in a strange foreign land. Most couldn't speak the language, and all had to deal with anti-immigrant discrimination.

Current defenders of illegal aliens like to say that they do the jobs that Americans won't do. What they really mean is that Americans won't do those jobs for excruciatingly long hours in exchange for criminally low wages. Both of my grandfathers, along with many other Italian immigrants at the time, went to the coal mines of Pennsylvania.

There they toiled in near darkness, performing back breaking labor, receiving just enough money to scrape by. When the long days were over they would trudge up from the depths of the Earth and have to deal with life in a society that didn't want them.

For most of the history of the United States, newly arrived ethnic groups had to fight their way up the social ladder to acceptance. The Irish, the Chinese, Jews and many others, including the Italians, came here in search of opportunity and while they found it, they had to contend with a lot of bigotry as well.

My maternal grandfather, Giuseppe Saurini, was a proud, hard working man and he had a rough time dealing with the discrimination that he had to endure on a daily basis. That, combined with the yearning he felt to be reunited with his family, led to his returning to Italy only a few years later.

My paternal grandfather, Pasquale Ferrari, also returned to the old country to see his family. While both of my grandfathers planned on returning to America, the outbreak of the First World War dashed those hopes. Still, the dream of America was kept alive in my family for the next generation.

Pasquale returned to his hometown of Sora, a small city of twenty thousand people situated near the Liri River in Italy. Large villas filled the city, with a main street so thriving that it rivaled the markets of Rome. Sora was a focal point of culture for the area and was the first city to have both an Opera house and a movie theatre. Their one day market was - and still is - the biggest in the county of Frosinone, the sounds and smells filling the town for miles around. Anything you could possibly want could be had there.

In the poor area of town, butting right up against the Appennine Mountains was where Pasquale Ferrari lived with his first born son Enrico - my father - and the rest of the family. They lived in a house that was meek, though it did have a thatched roof, which was a rarity at the time.

The mountains behind their house used to be home to the Carbonari, an underground army who once rebelled against the king. They got their name because they would cut down trees, cover them with dirt, and burn them to make coal, a trade which my grandfather inherited.

Seven miles away, in the town of Vicalvi, lived Maria Saurini. She grew up wealthier than Enrico, but was far from nobility. Her father, Giuseppe, was a land owner though, and that meant a lot. They may have been commoners, but they were a lot better off than the people around them.

Vicalvi was a farming village of less than a thousand people, which was founded back in 467 BC. Olive groves and vineyards surrounded the sun drenched hills. It was once the home of the Sannitis, who battled against the Romans during their early expansion. In 1070 AD the Normans built a castle to protect the town, which they controlled at the time, and later St. Francis of Assisi built a monastery there.

The Saurinis may have been wealthier than the Ferraris, but life for them was still hard. Running water was a luxury so Maria had to wash her family's laundry in the town fountain, balancing the wet clothing on her head on the way home.

Maria was the second youngest of five sisters. In a family with no brothers, her father had no choice but to make her and the other girls work out in the fields like men. The daughters, in addition to field work, were also responsible for the traditional female duties of the household. Unfortunately for her, Maria was the one who picked up all the slack. "Let Maria do it," was a common household phrase.

The first Saturday in October was the start of the three day "Feast for the Blessed Virgin Mary of the Rosary," held in Vicalvi. Although she's not the patron saint of Vicalvi, Italians have a very high regard for mothers and therefore the love they have for the mother of Jesus is seen as a reflection of the love they have for their own.

On Saturday afternoon a huge fireworks display announces the beginning of the feast. The days are filled with music and dancing and the streets are lit up and down with holiday illuminations, with big arches of lights. There are plenty of games and rides for the kids, such as the girandola - a personal favorite of the children.

The girandola consisted of a large wheel with seats hanging by chains and a hollow shaft in the middle. Inside the shaft were handles for the kids to hold on to, which they'd push to spin the ride.

The incentive for a free ride led to a lot of arguing and fighting over who got to do the pushing, which powered the ride. Once the seats got swinging, people would grab the chains of the people sitting in front of them before pulling them back and then kicking them forward. It was very simple but a lot of fun, the kids didn't need fancy lights or sound to get excited.

Sunday and Monday both have Processions of the Immaculate Conception and the Blessed Virgin Mother of the Rosary, respectively, ending with more fireworks. On Monday night the festival ends with the Feast of the Rosary. The feast concludes with a spectacular fireworks display, even grander than the previous ones.

The neighboring town holds the Feast of Santa Victoria on the same weekend, which has resulted in a rivalry based on who has the best fireworks. Every year the citizens of Vicalvi trick them by setting off what only appears to be a finale. The fireworks celebrating Santa Victoria are then set off, and when finished, Vicalvi sets off their real finale.

In 1931, Enrico was invited by friends from Vicalvi to attend the feast. He was so excited by the prospect that he finished a full day's work in only half the time. Despite his hard work, he almost missed the last bus to Vicalvi before it sped off.

He attended the religious festivities and was amazed by what he saw in the church. A special gold plated throne holds the Madonna statue for the procession. The throne is about ten feet high with four columns, one on each corner. The statue is set up on the throne with one hand holding the baby Jesus, and the other outstretched.

The throne is placed on an angled platform which sits high up on an altar almost at the top of the church. There are tracks hidden beneath and as the choir sings a special song honoring the Madonna, the platform begins to lower. The resulting effect makes it appear that the Virgin Mary is heading down to embrace you. It's quite a dramatic sight and people to this day who've never seen it before are amazed, some even moved to tears.

Emotions now stirred and stomach now empty, Enrico's friends took him to the Saurini's house to rest and eat. As Enrico walked through the door, there sat Maria preparing the meal. His jaw dropped. It was love at first sight. Of course, life is nothing without complications.

Already in the house was a young man from Vicalvi who was in the middle of courting Maria. Too hungry and exhausted to care, Enrico strode right through the house to a window overlooking the valley below to get some fresh air, lest he pass out. While outside recovering his breath he spied a pot of carnations hanging on the windowsill, one of which he picked, placing it into his lapel.

By the time that he returned inside, Maria's suitor had fled. He mistook Enrico's exhaustion for arrogance - who did he think he was to just stroll into a stranger's house and pick their flowers? It may not sound like much, but back then that was a big liberty to take. The young man assumed that Enrico must have been a big shot and didn't think that he could compete, so he left.

Now feeling like he was the happiest - and possibly luckiest - man alive, Enrico made arrangements to return the following Sunday and continue the courting.

Italian courtship is very strict, much more so back in those days. Even when a couple danced a handkerchief was held between the man and woman. The couple was also never left alone, there was always someone with them, usually a relative.

The whole courting process was for the purpose of marriage, not recreation. Love was seen as more of a practical thing. It was felt that if you were genuine and honest with each other as a couple, that you'd learn to love each other even if you didn't at the time.

When a couple was courting it was the opportunity for the woman's family to judge the man - was he honest and respectful? Was he a good worker and provider? How would he help the family? What was his demeanor like? And so on.

Prior to meeting Enrico, Maria was engaged to another man. One day while she was making tomato paste - a very laborious process - her fiancé stopped by to talk to her. As soon as he saw that she was wearing the ring that he gave her while working the paste he started to complain. Maria immediately pulled the ring off of her finger and threw it at him. The fact that he felt that it was more important to keep his ring nice and shiny than it was to appreciate all her hard work meant that he wasn't husband material.

In contrast, Enrico was a true gentleman and only two months after they first met, he and Maria were wed. The ceremonies were very structured and bound by traditional rituals back then. A week before the wedding, Le Commarelles - who were equivalent to bridesmaids - would each decorate a basket, fill them full of linens and go from the bride's house to the groom's carrying them and everything else that the bride would need to be set up in her new home. The more Le Commarelles that a bride had, the bigger the dowry was.

The traditions of the time also meant that the wedding would be made up only of fifteen to thirty close family members and that they would be married in the bride's church, with the feast and reception at the bride's home. And knowing Giuseppe, the reception had plenty of food and plenty of wine.

It's not even an issue today, but at the time it was a big deal that my mother was marrying a man from another town. Enrico, because he was so poor, moved in with the Saurinis and began to work for his father-in-law Giuseppe as a sharecropper. The newlyweds worked all day together out in the fields, and at night Enrico and the men would take care of the farm animals, while the women would head inside and prepare the night's meal over a wood fire.

It was a simple farming life. When the sun set they went to sleep, and when it rose they woke up and went to work. During mid-day, when the sun was at its peak and it became too hot to work, they'd take their break.

All this hard work began to take its toll on Maria's back, but she always worked regardless of the pain. Even after giving birth to each of her six children, she'd be right back to work only days later. She always took care of her family and always kept a positive outlook on life. She continues to pray every day of her life, right up till her present age of 98. She taught her family to always do good things, right things, and often told them stories of their family's history.

Enrico was an enterprising man and the poor life of a sharecropper was not for him. To earn extra money he began to take trips to Rome. Maria would take over his farm chores as he took the only form of transportation available to him - his bicycle.

He'd bike the seventy-five miles up to Rome and spend months working there before returning home with his money. Then he began to bring back goods - whatever he could find at a good price - and sell them back in Vicalvi. He used the money he earned to begin to buy land from his father in-law.

"Land" may be a misnomer. It was more like he bought a piece of rock. The land was right up against the mountainside, but no mere mountain was going to stop Enrico. With nothing more than a pick and shovel he broke up the sections of loose rock, then used dynamite to level the ground.

It took a long time to get the land the way he wanted it, but Enrico had a gift to be able to visualize exactly what he wanted, and sculpted reality to fit his dreams. Once he got his land flat enough, he began building a home for himself, Maria, and the family that they planned to start. The trench for his home's foundation was dug right into the rock below.

In only three years Enrico saved up so much money that the townspeople began to borrow money from him. It was quite an accomplishment for him to be better off than most of the landowners in Vicalvi because he had started with nothing, and he could now help out his friends by loaning them the money that they needed.

Once he had money, he began to buy property. His wallet may have been growing, but for Enrico, money did not equal wealth. He taught his children that wealth isn't really money, real wealth is the family. Wealth is in having a family that is together. It's in having a family that appreciates other family members. It's much better for the soul to be wealthy in love than in money.

Earning what's adequate to provide wealth for your family - that's true happiness. And if you have that type of mentality and you're entrepreneurial and living in America, you'll earn a lot of money as well.

Chapter 2

As Enrico and Maria started their family, things in Italy began to change. By the time their first two children were born - Anna Igida and Ortensia, Benito Mussolini had come to power. When my brother Pasquale was born in 1936, Mussolini was attempting to create goodwill and a strong sense of nationality amongst the Italian people. Prizes were being awarded for everything that you could possibly imagine - Best Sheep, Best Livestock and even Healthiest Baby, for which Pasquale won the prize for in Vicalvi, much to Maria's pride.

Naturally no one knew at the time that Mussolini would wind up becoming the worst thing to happen to Italy since the fall of the Roman Empire. His alliance with the Nazis brought nothing but horror to Sora, Vicalvi and the other poor farming villages near Monte Cassino.

In my family, I'm the second youngest and the rest of my siblings, with the exception of my younger sister, were all born before or during the war. Growing up I got to know the sacrifices that they made.

To this day in Vicalvi the Americans and their military are always spoken of with glowing accolades, while the Nazis who occupied the town during the war are spoken of with nothing but pure hatred.

The area of Monte Cassino near Vicalvi was considered by the Allies to be the lynchpin to Rome. St. Benedict's monastery was at the top of the mountainside, making it a very strategic location. Whoever controlled it controlled the pass that leads into the Valley di Comino and the Liri Valley.

Upon entering Vicalvi, the Nazis marched up to the Norman castle, which with six foot thick walls was a literal fortress, and forced out the native people. They took the castle for themselves while leaving the townspeople exposed and homeless.

With the castle occupied, they painted a red cross on the southern exposure so that the Allied Forces, who were moving north, would think that it was a field hospital. They were hoping that the airplanes bombing the area would avoid hitting it, and instead concentrate on the town below.

At the start of the war, the Ferraris had three children. Enrico was soon drafted, leaving Maria to run the household and take care of the children by herself. In the 1920s he had worked in the military as a chauffeur. Due to his previous service and his ability to read and write, he was able to avoid the chaos of the front lines and instead was made an interpreter and stationed in Rome.

There he read letters that were moving back and forth between soldiers and their families. He would translate the regional dialects so that the commanders could decide what needed to be redacted.

In 1943 his fourth child, my sister Concetta, was born and he was sent home. Mussolini felt that a family with four or more children should have their father with them, so when my father found out that my mother was pregnant he was able to return to Vicalvi. When he arrived he found that life was almost more bearable in the military. By that point the power lines had been destroyed beyond repair and Vicalvi had no electricity.

It was the middle of the night when Maria felt the undeniable signs of labor. She woke Enrico and told him to take the other children to their grandmother's house at the top of the hill, and bring back her mother to help with the birth. Enrico agreed and left with the children.

There, alone in the darkness, the baby started to arrive. Unable to wait for her mother's return, Maria gave birth to her daughter Concetta right there on the floor of her home. Reaching around in the pitch black, she was able to find one of her dresser drawers. Pulling it open she felt for a pair of scissors. Finding them, she used them to cut the umbilical cord. After tying it off, she found a piece of fabric for the baby and wrapped her in it. When Enrico returned he was startled to hear a baby's cries.

Vicalvi being a farming community, a lot of men were exempt from duty because they had four or more kids. The Nazis, however, didn't care. Rather than risk their own lives, they took the Italian civilians to the front lines to dig trenches. My youngest sister Loreta lost the man who was to be her godfather because he was taken out to the front lines and killed while digging.

Any able-bodied man that could be found was forcibly abducted and taken into the war zone. It didn't matter that they weren't in the military or that most had no training at all. The Nazis needed dangerous work done and because of what some would call arrogance, and others cowardice, used the Italians as their slave labor.

Once the death toll began piling up, the men in the town began to go into hiding. Enrico knew he'd be taken if caught, so he grabbed a shovel and dug a cave into the mountainside behind his house. Lugging an old large wine barrel to the cave, he buried it underneath the dirt to provide himself with an entrance to his shelter. He then hid the entrance to the barrel with a large rock. To further disguise the barrel he covered it in soil and planted vegetables right on top of it. It was in this tiny shelter that he lived for many months.

The Ferrari children believed that their father had left them, but each night under the cover of darkness, Enrico would sneak back into the house to be with his wife. It pained them both to keep this secret from their children. They knew their kids were simply too young to be trusted and might unknowingly blurt out the secret in front of the Nazis.

Concetta was the one exception, but only for the first few months of his hiding. As she grew older she began to show excitement when in the vicinity of her father's hiding spot and would start pointing. Sadly, the joy of seeing Enrico was the reason why she no longer could. Afraid that she might inadvertently give away his hideout in front of the wrong people, the decision was made to keep the baby away from her father.

While Concetta was still a baby, an Austrian Nazi captain fell in love with her. She had blue eyes, and looked very Aryan, just like the little boy that he had lost back home.

As Maria came home one day, she stepped into the empty house. It was quiet, except for the giggling of her daughter. She entered her room and found the captain crouched down on the floor, playing with her baby.

The Nazi smiled, stood, and walked out. Maria was chilled to the bone. At any time he wanted, the captain could come in and take her child as his own. If they tried to stop him, they'd be killed in cold blood.

Because of these horrors, my father had an escape route planned out. He even kept a backpack that he measured to ensure that my sister could fit.

As the war wore on, the thunder cracks of exploding bombs became a daily occurrence, but the day to day life of the townspeople had to continue. Maria and her family kept working in the fields, as the only other choice was starvation.

The attacks were so frequent that when the bombs began going off, she and the other farmers were able to judge the distance and work right up until the last second before having to evacuate and seek shelter.

Enrico was proud that throughout the war, despite the starving conditions of the town, he was always able to feed his family white bread. That may not sound like much, but bread was a scarce commodity. Like most families, the Ferraris didn't have a lot of food to go around, but they had enough to at least fill the bellies around the table, which was much more than most.

Still, it remained a fairly meager existence. During the day the children would scavenge through the fields for edible herbs and weeds, and grab small animals like snails for protein. As the war wore on, the desperation of the townspeople grew.

One family was known as the Famiglia della Coperta, i.e. the Blanket Family. They didn't have enough clothes for the winter so they would share the one blanket that they owned and took turns going outside. And they, like most families affected by the war began dreaming of a better life in America.

Even the meager amount of crops that the families were able to farm was taken from them. Once the shadow of the Nazis came over the village, all farmers were ordered to take everything that they harvested to the mill. Grains that were brought to the mill were confiscated by the Nazi war machine. It was not the property of those who grew it; it all belonged to the greater glory of the Third Reich.

In exchange for their hard work, the townspeople were rewarded with a slip of paper to be used for rations. After they received their ration slip, their food was confiscated by the government and sent to the soldiers on the front lines. Even after the Italian government stopped the practice, the Nazis continued to take what they wished and gave nothing back.

Vicalvi may not have been a wealthy community before the war, but the people were at least allowed to keep what they worked so hard to grow.

For the Ferraris to provide for their family, they would keep their wheat hidden. In the dead of night they ground the grain in their coffee grinder under a blanket, little by little, enough to make some bread, make some pasta, and feed the kids.

There was never enough food to go around. Meat was saved for holidays as no one could afford to kill livestock. Most families had only one or two cows - no one had enough livestock to constitute a herd. They would rather have a cow keep producing milk, or a chicken keep producing eggs then kill the animal for one meal. The Nazis, however, didn't care.

One couple in the nearby village of Santo Padre owned a donkey that the Nazis wanted. The husband was trying the make them understand that his donkey was the only way he had to support his family and get the work done in the fields. As the argument grew more and more heated, the Nazi soldiers decided to end it the only way they knew how. Drawing their weapons, the soldiers shot the couple both dead and then took the donkey.

Enrico heard about the cold blooded murders and when he saw the Nazis trying to take a chicken from his friend Luciano, he bravely stepped in. Luciano tried to explain to the soldiers that he needed the chicken to provide eggs. If they killed it for a single meal he would starve.

Enrico saw one of the soldiers reach for his weapon and grabbed his friend. He made Luciano give up his chicken. Luciano was angry until Enrico explained that it was either the chicken or his life.

Nazi patrols would head through town often, and God forbid they heard something suspicious. The Nazis purposely built up suspicion between the townspeople, so you never knew who was loyal to Mussolini or the Nazis or to the townspeople.

Years after the fact, our neighbor Tomaso Vitella, told me about a night during the war when he heard something outside and saw some shadows near the barn. He had thought that his cows had gotten out, but when he went to see what was going on, he found five Jews hiding from the Nazis.

Despite knowing that he's be executed if the Nazis found out that he was helping Jews, he went into the house and got them half a loaf of bread and let them stay in the barn. After he went back inside his house he didn't say a word about the incident to anyone, not even his wife.

Life was tough, miserable and dangerous, and the war was especially hard on the children. Enrico's oldest son, Pasquale, named after his grandfather, would often go to the Nazi's portable kitchen with a pail to beg for scraps of food, taking whatever he got home to share with his family.

Terrified that something might happen to them, my parents decided to take their life savings and bury them under a cherry tree. They knew that they couldn't tell their children about the money in case they said something inadvertently, so instead they told the kids that if the two of them had ever met with a tragic accident, they should go and dig under the cherry tree. If they dug deep enough they would see their parents again.

Of course that wasn't true, but if they dug deep enough then they would find the money intended for them. I may not have lived through those times, but when I hear things like that, it really brings a lot of emotions out. It's hard to even imagine what those people had to go through - the suffering. It really allows one to appreciate what you have in life, and by the grace of God, are able to accumulate and enjoy and pass on to your family.

As the war reached its climax, there was no infrastructure left in the town. Corpses of those killed in the Allied attacks

- both the townspeople and the Nazis - were sometimes left in the streets. As the Allies got closer and closer, surrounding towns were forced to evacuate by the Nazis before the inevitable battle. There was no order. Whoever was put on the truck was evacuated. Families were divided, with children crying for their parents as they were driven off.

The day before the citizens of Vicalvi prepared to evacuate themselves, the Allied forces broke through, bombing the main road to Rome and preventing the Nazi's evacuation trucks from coming through. A week later the Allies - specifically the Americans - drove out the occupying Nazis and were welcomed with open arms.

The Americans were the good guys, liberating the oppressed citizens from Hitler's thugs. Women hung their white sheets outside their windows as a sign of peace. The townspeople ran through the streets crying "freedom."

They were glad that it was the Americans who liberated them because the Americans treated the Italians well. The Moroccan Army was also fighting in Italy, but their role in the liberation was hardly a thing to celebrate. They were terrible, even going so far as to rape the women of the freed towns.

But the Americans brought food and clothing. They rebuilt the buildings and churches. There were a few things that the Americans wanted - like good home cooked meals, which were still hard to come by, even after the liberation, but I don't blame them for that. Even so, they were more than happy to offer a chocolate bar for a good meal. Even their toothpaste tasted like candy.

With the town free, the Ferraris went and unearthed their money from under the cherry tree. The container they used wasn't waterproof, so they hung their paper money out to dry over a wood fire. It was the beginning of a new life.

With the war over, things began to slowly get better. Italy took almost twenty years to recover from the war and a lot of people wanted to leave and seek a better life. The United

States helped a lot to reestablish order in Italy and touched everyone's lives.

America sacrificed to help Europe get out from under the yoke of Hitler and Mussolini. America was the white knight that came to help not only the other European countries that had been occupied by Hitler, but also Italy, which, because Mussolini joined forces with Hitler, was an enemy of the United States.

I grew up hearing about how the Americans came to help win the war. Those are sacrifices that, thank God, I don't remember, because I wasn't born until a month before the end of the war. There still wasn't much to go around at first, but my family eventually recovered.

During the war, my parents, Enrico and Maria, and my older brother and sisters, Anna, Ortensia, Pasquale, and Concetta lived through daily horrors and they all waited for the day that the Americans would come. Once they did, the people of Vicalvi had a little bit of freedom, a little bit of relief and hearing these stories really helped me formulate my opinion about America.

Chapter 3

While the Allied Forces were making their final push to end the war, so too was my mother giving her final push to bring me into the world. I was born in April of 1945, only a month before the war ended. I may not have been alive for the trials that the rest of my family endured, but growing up during the postwar reconstruction had its own share of hardships

While my childhood may have been hard, what was most important was the stories that my family told me about the Americans, and the efforts of their soldiers. They were our liberators, our heroes, our saviors.

We all knew the sacrifices that the Americans had gone through to liberate us, and so in the post-war years everyone wanted to come to America. Even at the turn of the century when there was a lot of ethnic bigotry, Italians were still migrating to America to make a better life for themselves. My entire life I was surrounded by the desire to immigrate overseas.

I cannot stress it enough when I say - I loved America before I ever set foot upon it. As a child I heard about all the brave things that the Americans did to free my people. I started to want America, I started to crave America.

I do, however, find it necessary to point out that our family's quest for a better life in America shouldn't be mistaken for a hatred of Italy, or wished any ill will towards our motherland. It was the harsh conditions of a post-war economy that drove many Italians to immigrate elsewhere.

My family's appreciation for America's part in World War II and for the life that it offered was the ultimate motivator. I'm happy to say that with the help of America, Italy is now again one of the major world economies and tourists consider it to be a highly desired country to visit.

After the war, things were in disarray. Even with the Nazis gone, life could still be dangerous. Unexploded bombs were being found in the fields, and the American soldiers had to be called to take care of them.

In one incident, half the town was gathered around a bomb, tense and nervous, anxiously awaiting the Bomb Squad. When the guy from the Bomb Squad came, he looked it over, picked it up, put it under his arm and just walked right off, as if it was nothing. We were all impressed by his nonchalant bravery.

Poverty was rampant, so people looked to migrate to other countries that could offer them a better life and better opportunities. America was everyone's goal. America was the shining cup. It was where everyone wanted to live.

Things from America were prized. My brother-in-law's brother Palmino once received a hooded jacket that was sent to him from a relative in the US. He was instantly the envy of the town.

One day an immigrant came home from the States with his 1954 Dodge. To this day I vividly remember the two tone paint job of light green and dark. It was some car to see. Maybe it's because I'm a Ferrari, but I've always loved cars.

Italian cars were fine, but American cars were larger and more luxurious, even the horn made a richer sound.

Tales about America began to circulate - like stories of gold flowing in the street. Of course those stories dated all the way back to the Gold Rush a hundred years earlier, but a lot of things that were said were always very positive about what one could achieve by attaining a life in America.

I was shocked by tales of the abundance in America. We heard that there was so much to go around, and Americans had so much to eat that Americans would even throw out their food. That kind of thing was unheard of - nobody threw out food! But America was the land of plenty, on the table there was always plenty. There was so much that the excess would just be thrown out.

In fact, I don't think I ever heard a single bad thing said about America. Certainly there were differences - religion for one. I knew that other religions existed, but everyone I knew was Roman Catholic. In America there was no Catholic prayer to start the school day, because you were free to pursue whatever religion you wished.

There was also a lot of ethnic diversity, which was something that we didn't see much of where I grew up - before leaving for America I only saw a single black person! In America there were many races and ethnicities and all were looked at as equal under the law.

There were some people who remembered when my grandparents had gone to America and returned with tales of Italians not being treated very well, but that was a long time ago and a lot had changed.

What I heard about America was that no matter where someone started, they could become well-off. They worked, they made good wages and most importantly, had freedom and could get an education. Even a commoner, even a poor person could rise high in the ranks of politics or become wealthy in business as long as they gave it their all.

Those were the stories I heard. Sure, they were embellished at times, but that was our perception of such a great country. The perception was that all Americans had large luxurious automobiles and that every home had a television. In my entire hometown there were only two television sets. That was it. Most people had radios, but not everyone - my family didn't.

Our lives were meager, but we were blessed. We didn't have a car, just my father's bicycle, or there was always the donkey. We weren't living on a dirt floor, our floor was cement, but there was no carpeting or hardwood or anything like that. Our home had a fireplace and all the things that we needed. As my father continued to save up money we eventually bought a two-burner stove with a butane tank. That was when we knew we hit the big time - that was luxury!

Before the stove we had to cook everything over the crackling flame of the fireplace. We didn't mind so much in the winter, but during the long hot summers, it meant that there was no shelter from the heat. The stove made things a lot easier, especially for my mother.

We had no running water either. If we wanted water we carried a barrel to the fountain a block and a half away, filled it up and lugged it back home.

I had no toys, nor a bicycle, just an old bike rim that I played with. My sisters didn't have any dolls or a tea set. If someone broke a dish, they'd get to use the pieces to play with. I know now that it wasn't much, but I never complained. I had fun with what I had.

We didn't even have power lines when I was a child, as it took a while for them to be repaired following the war. We read and studied by the flickering fire, and were in bed soon after dark, and then up before sunrise. At night we'd sit around with each other and read stories. We had a lot of family time together, which built a strong bond that remains to this day. I would advise all families to set aside some time each day and be together; it builds a lot of character.

Because we didn't have any electricity when I was a child, much like the pioneers, I had to read and do my homework by candlelight. Money was sometimes so tight that I couldn't even use the single candle that we had for long periods of time because we needed to conserve it.

At the time, I didn't think too much about it, it was just the way things were, and as far as I knew, had always had been. The day started with a prayer and ended with a prayer and we thanked God for all the things that we had. There were never any complaints about the things that we didn't. It was a comfort knowing that there was a better life out there that other people were enjoying, because we knew in our hearts that some day we would be enjoying it too.

As a child, I was raised to respect my elders - we all were. Every old man was referred to as Uncle, and every old lady was Aunt. That was just out of respect. Old age is revered in Italy, because old age means one thing - experience. Every day you learn something new, so every day is a learning experience. Someone who has lived a long life is someone you council with. I would never go and council with people that were in their thirties or forties, I would go and council with someone who was much older.

It was an honor to ask an elder for their council. They gave back to their community. They didn't write a check, they just gave their knowledge and sometimes the greatest thing that we can do to give back is to just pass on our knowledge. It is such a powerful tool.

I think it's tragic that in this country old age is looked down upon. Here people say, "I'm still 39." They make jokes that they never get old. In Italy it's an honor to be old. If I asked my father how old he was, if he had just completed his 60th birthday, he would say, "I'm 61 years old."

And I would say, "Papa, you just started 60."

He'd say, "No, 60 is gone, I'm in my 61st year."

That was the way that we looked at the years of life. It was an honor to be older because older meant you should be wiser and by and large it followed that design - the older you are, the more experience, the more knowledge you have. So when you go and talk to an older person, you can get their knowledge, they will pass it on to you.

My father lived to be almost 94 years old. My mother, God bless her, is still alive and sharp at 98, and to this day I talk to her every Sunday. I call, talk, and see how she's doing. I was taught to always respect old-age.

My father worked hard, and pushed my family to work hard, but for good reason. He wanted everyone to do all we could to make our lives better. He wanted to make things better at home, just in case he wasn't able bring his family to America. There was always a Plan B with my father.

I idolized my father to the point that when I started school I made sure that my hair was combed just like his. I had a picture of him from when he was in the Army and I would make sure that my hair was combed the exact same way.

During dinner, when my dish was filled at meal time it had to be the same as my father's or I wouldn't eat. I didn't even want to go to bed before my father did. Of course, I would always fall asleep by the fire and sometimes to tease me, my father would get up and pretend to leave and I'd wake up and scream that my father was gone.

My father was a very enterprising man. He was very proud that the farm land which he owned was bought, not inherited. He worked very hard to buy the land, and aside from working the fields of our family farm, he also owned a grocery store in town.

After the war it was hard to attain goods. My father discovered that he could purchase goods in Rome for a lower price, and then take them home and sell them at a profit. There was only one problem - Rome was over seventy miles away and in order to get there you had to travel through the mountains. And remember - we didn't have a car, only a bicycle.

To my father this was not an obstacle, merely a challenge. It was a treacherous trek, but he would ride his bicycle to Rome, making it there over the course of several days.

The return trip took even longer. He'd load up his goods on the bicycle, and so there was no room for him to ride, so he had to walk it back. It was hard, but my father always prided himself that while there wasn't an abundance of food, his kids were never hungry.

While my father was gone we would run the store. Three days a week we would hold an open market in the surrounding towns. We all knew what we had to do to keep things running.

Our store was a one room space and was set up on the main street that led to Rome. It had a big arched door at the entrance, but was very plain inside, just four walls, no decorative stuff. After the war people didn't care about things like that, they just wanted to come in and get whatever they could buy that they needed.

There was a counter at one end with shelves with different types of pasta and canned goods. On another one was goods that could be used for rope, and farming utensils, but we mainly sold pasta and dry goods.

Our store was very popular and all the townspeople knew exactly when we were going to be open. My father set up a table and some chairs and sometimes people would come in to play a game of cards. It wasn't like a bar or anything, but our store became somewhat of a gathering place for the local people.

The entire time that my father was saving to buy up property for us to live on, he was also putting aside money so that he could afford to move our family to America. Because of the war, the lira was devalued such an extent that it was practically worthless. Before the war one lira was about equal to one dollar. By the 1950s it took almost 700 lira to equal a single buck. The devaluation was unbelievable but he still saved up enough to pay someone to sponsor him to come over.

In fact he wasn't able to save up enough money to come to the United States. Instead he was able to get sponsored to come to Canada. It wasn't the prized America - but it was still North America.

He had to pay 240,000 lira to get sponsored. That was a lot of money, but when you have six children it doesn't really go all that far. When some of the townspeople heard that he had paid 240,000 lira to a neighbor who was already in Canada, just to get sponsored to go, they smirked and said that if they had 240,000 lira they would stay in Italy and live like a king.

My father replied, "How do you live like a king with six children? How long can you live like a king? But if I have my opportunity I hope to have my children live in a good way in America."

He was still building our house and trying to improve living conditions while saving up all this money. He wanted to have the house finished before he left for Canada, and we all chipped in to make his dreams - our dreams - a reality.

We all sacrificed to come to this country. My older siblings really sacrificed their childhoods and teenage years working to make ends meet. I was able to continue on to high school and college, while most of my siblings were unable to.

Being able to afford to come to America was only the first hurdle. There were many more obstacles between our first being sponsored to come over and our actual arrival.

Chapter 4

I would travel with my father during his efforts to secure our passage to America. First we would travel by bus to Frosinone, the county seat, then later by train to Rome, and lastly to Naples for final immigration approval.

It was a special time for me to be traveling with my father. When we took the train to Naples we would go past Monte Cassino. I was only five years old at the time, but I distinctly remember seeing rows and rows of white crosses along the hillside.

Curious, I asked my father about them. There, over the rhythmic clacking of the train as it hurtled along the tracks, he explained to me that those were the graves of American soldiers who fought valiantly to liberate Europe from the crushing grip of the Nazis.

Those trips were my first memories of hearing about the exploits of the Americans during the war and what they did, and what they went through to help us. Every journey past those crosses reinforced my feeling about how incredible American soldiers and citizens were, and how America was behind the

29

efforts to free the Europeans. Every trip my appreciation grew for what the Americans did for others, myself included.

It was a real awakening - or as much as an awakening as you can have as a five year old boy. It began my understanding of the dream that was America. Everyone on that train had the same dream. Each was dreaming of starting a new life in the land of opportunity. That land would help them provide for their parents, and provide for their children, who like me would grow up enjoying the benefits of their parents' sacrifices.

Throughout these trips we were herded along like cattle and placed in cavernous rooms to sleep. The men and women were separated from one another. It was very uncomfortable to be split from the rest of the family.

We spent three days in Naples getting medical and mental tests. You had to be in good health both mentally and physically, and couldn't have a criminal record. The officials spoke to the local priests and policemen to make sure that each family was on the up and up.

We avoided talking to people, because some of them were selfish and because only a limited amount of people were approved, they would try to prevent others from getting a visa.

In the evenings, while waiting in the large rooms, the men and women would join in prayer. They fervently prayed that their wish would be granted and that they'd receive final approval to come to the United States. At such a young age it overwhelmed me to see all those grownups praying to come to America.

Among those prayers there was a lot of sadness. Families would sometime break down in tears because one of their children was sick. The entire family had to be in good health in order to be approved. If even one family member had a minor disability, or even a small disfigurement like a bad finger then they would be turned down, and they'd miss out on the golden opportunity of America.

For those who didn't make it and weren't approved to come over, it was a great sadness. They had just experienced going through the horror of World War II, only to be turned down for a visa. It was very hard to take, but the people had a lot of resolve and they persevered.

But as depressing as it could be at times, it was ultimately a joyous occasion, because we all knew that most of us would have much to celebrate when it was all over.

When a family did get approval it was a very joyous event, but it could also be heart wrenching because that also meant that there would be a separation. Usually the whole family wouldn't be in a position to just pick up and leave. They wouldn't have the money or the resources, so usually the father and maybe one of the older siblings would leave first.

The days were filled with nervous anticipation. We watched the reactions of other families as they were either approved - resulting in joyous celebrations - or rejected - resulting in heart wrenching sadness. A single slip of paper determined the whole rest of your life.

Time itself seemed to slow for us, so much was riding on our approval. Then one day it happened. A man came to us with our notice, stamped with approval. All the years of hardship, all of the struggle and the sacrifice broke right then and there.

After getting approval in Naples we rode back with families that were celebrating and families that were devastated. It was a very mixed bag of joyous people and people in deep sadness. We all felt really sad for the families who didn't make it. They were crying the whole way home.

Our news began to spread throughout the town. A lot of the folks who earlier said that they would stay in Italy and live like kings had a tab running at my father's grocery store. When my father left, that tab never got paid, because they said that he was an American now, and so he didn't need their money.

Years later my father threw away the book, telling them, "God bless you all and I hope everyone is doing well. I certainly don't need the money so I hope it went for a good cause."

And I'm sure it did because most of the people that owed money to him used it to buy food, and nothing else.

I soon learned that we wouldn't be traveling as a family to America. Rather, only my father could afford to go. As he gained a foothold and began building his new life, he would begin to send for my older siblings, and eventually my mother, my younger siblings and I. We didn't know how long it would be, though most certainly years.

The thought of losing my father was devastating. It was a terrible hardship having our family separated, but it was for a good cause. We always knew that we'd eventually reunite in the United States and our lives would all be better for it.

It was especially hard on me when my father left. He was my whole world. I shed a lot of tears, but they weren't all in sadness. I would write letters to him while he was in Canada and would wait everyday for his letters back. Even decades later, after my father retired and moved back to Italy, I still called him on the phone at least once a week, every week.

The day that my father left for America, I got up early and had to go to school, though I can't say I learned much that day. I could see our new house from the school window, and tried to watch my father all day. The second the school day was over, I bolted straight home, where my family was gathered.

Before my father left he made sure that the first story of our house was finished. He wanted the rest of our family to be situated in our own home on our own land. He had the whole thing timed out perfectly, though quite close. He literally finished hanging the last of the doors and left for America.

He never even got to sleep in the finished home that he had worked so hard to build.

We were all crying and smiling all at the same time - happy that he was going, but sad that he was leaving. My family was filled with hope for the future, but it was heartbreaking all the same. And not just for our family, but for the townspeople as well.

It was scary for him leaving as it was for us having him leave. He didn't speak any English or even know anyone except for a few people in Toronto. He was leaving our family behind, but was doing it to earn a better life for everyone. And so he sacrificed and his wishes came true.

A man showed up from a car service to take him to the port, and so with a suitcase for himself, and a second with goods to bring to other immigrants in Canada, he loaded up his things. It was tearful, joyous time. His final instructions to me were to be good and listen to my mother.

I looked up at him smiling, eyes still swollen with tears. It seemed almost unreal that he was leaving. As the car door shut, I stood huddled with my family. We didn't know when we'd be together again, but we all knew that our American dream was finally beginning.

Chapter 5

When my father left, he left a void not only for me as a father figure, but also as the head of the household. Within a short period of time, however, we managed to adapt. My mother was already used to helping to do my father's duties both during the war as well as during my father's long trips to Rome. Our whole family fell into place doing their daily work. Places and chores were assumed and done. We all knew that my father would be gone, so we all stepped up.

My older siblings worked the fields and farmed on a daily basis so that we could not only feed ourselves, but take product to market. Everything we did was based on trying to provide for ourselves. Age didn't matter; everyone kept working just the same whether my father was there or not.

My sister Concetta, who was only ten at the time, mostly worked out in the fields, but she would also take the time to come into our house and make the lunchtime meal. Once she was done cooking, she'd gather up everything, balance it on her head and carry it out to us.

She was a very nurturing person, and so she was also put in charge of the livestock. When our sow would have a litter of piglets, she'd fatten them up for market and they were always the first to be sold.

With my father gone, my brother Pasquale was now the eldest male in the home, and according to Italian tradition, was now considered head of the household. I had always looked up to him; he loved me very much and always looked out for me, and because he was now in charge, my admiration and respect only increased.

When he turned fourteen, Pasquale wanted to go to Rome to work because you could make a better wage working there as a migrant farm worker picking wheat. Every day he would head into town to meet up with the older guys as they headed off on their trips, but they didn't want to take him because he was too young.

Much like my father, he was persistent and kept showing up day after day, pushing them to take him along. The men grew to admire the perseverance coming from such a young boy and eventually they relented and began taking him with them to Rome.

Pasquale was extremely proud to finally be taken seriously as an adult. He worked hard in Rome and the income that he earned there gave us a good deal of monetary relief.

Even though my father was gone, work on our house kept going, courtesy of my oldest sister Anna. While my father may have finished our house enough for us to live in, he still had a list of improvements and so she kept working to finish our home the way he wanted.

This went beyond simply carpentry. Part of my father's plans included another stable for the animals, which meant that more of the mountainside had to be leveled. Though it was hard work, Anna took a certain pleasure drilling holes in the rocks behind our house, filling them with dynamite to level them off.

She wanted to get the job done as quickly as possible so she would pack in as much powder as she could. The explosions would blow the rocks high into the air. As kids we thought it was an incredible sight, but our neighbor wasn't so enthusiastic. Once the rocks were blown so far that they hit the clay roof of his home while he was inside. Screaming like a maniac, he came running out the house - he thought he'd been blasted by a bomb!

Over in Canada my father was having a rough time. As soon as he arrived in Toronto he began to look for work. Although he had accomplished many extraordinary things while in Italy, none of it mattered in the New World, it was like he was living underground all over again. He had to start his life all over again.

It was hard for him to assimilate. The Canadian lifestyle was totally different from what he was used to in Italy, and he had to deal with a lot of fear and discrimination. This was only six years after the war, and some Canadians still didn't like the Italians, who were so recently their enemies. Mussolini used to say that his soldiers were like lions. He claimed that they were so fierce that they would actually eat people. Some of these people actually took him at his word and thought that Italians were cannibalistic!

Those factors contributed a lot to his struggle to find a job, and he was also stifled by the language barrier. He had to settle for odd jobs and eventually found a basement apartment to live in while he looked for something steady.

As the months wore on, work remained scarce, and my father wasn't able to send too much money home to us because he was trying to save every scrap he had so that he could reunite the family in America. Eventually he heard that there was work in Sarnia, and because he wasn't finding any luck in Toronto, he, along with a few other immigrants he had met, decided to move there and booked train passage.

The Italian stigma was still with them when they disembarked, and it was very hard to find room and board.

Luckily my father met a Polish couple who took him in, and would later do the same for my brother and sister.

They lived in Bluewater, which is about a forty minute walk to downtown Sarnia. Located at the bottom tip of Lake Huron, Sarnia is now one of the largest cities on the lake, but in the fifties, Sarnia was a small town of around thirty thousand people. It was right on the border, with a bridge - called both the Bluewater and Sarnia Bridge - which led to Port Heron in America. To this day it's one of the busiest border crossings in Canada. There was a lot of activity going on for such a small town.

My father arrived right at Sarnia's boom time. Oil had been discovered and so several refineries were being built, and Dow Chemical was building a plant there as well in what's now known as Chemical Valley. All of this meant lot of construction work, which in turn meant lots of work for immigrants.

Sarnia being a small town, the downtown area was really only about two streets - Front and Christina. For about six blocks along the street are shops and there are also two theatres, though at the time there was only one. It seemed like the town was changing almost daily as more and more immigrants continued to pour in, most of whom were Italian. Having such a large and growing Italian population also meant that the discrimination soon dissolved.

There was also an Indian reservation nearby. When my father first told me about it I didn't quite understand why the Indians had to live on the reservation because after all, it was their country first. I also didn't understand why they couldn't buy whisky.

At the time in Canada you had to have a special permit to buy alcohol. It was hard for me to comprehend why the Indians had to beg Italians and other Caucasians to buy them whiskey. Some people took even more advantage of them by charging them extra so that they could turn a profit. My father even knew one guy who was unemployed and made all his money buying whiskey for the Indians.

So my father and his friends soon found the work that they'd been looking for. On Saturdays my father would wait for the bus into town with the other Italian men who lived and worked in Bluewater. My father, who at only about five foot five had pretty short legs, was a fast walker and energetic all his life. Usually, once the bus came, he would say good bye to his friends as they got on the bus, and would choose to walk instead.

The other men would laugh and say "You know, Enrico, with all the time you spend walking, you're gonna wear out the soles of your shoes. For only ten cents you can ride with us."

He would reply, "Ah, by the time you guys get there, you'll have waited here and then you've got to wait there to come back," he says, "I'll get there about the same time you do."

And he would in fact get there around the same time that the bus got there and more importantly, he'd save his dime. He'd save his dime going, and even when he had stuff to carry back to Bluewater, he would only take the bus back sometimes.

One of my uncles once asked him how he saved up all his money to buy his four bedroom house. My father answered by saying, "From all those dimes I saved every time I walked instead of taking the bus."

Sure, it was a little more than those dimes, but my uncle got the joke and my father got his vindication in one fell swoop. That's the kind of guy my father was. He saved, and sacrificed and worked hard all his life to provide for his family. Really, that's all he ever wished for.

Chapter 6

After about a year of constant struggle my father was finally able to secure a job in construction. He worked for over six months, saving up money, and waiting to see if his new job would be steady. Once he felt that things were solidifying, and that he had a decent place to live, he sponsored Anna and Pasquale to come and join him in Canada.

We were excited to hear the news, even if it meant another split for our family. Anna and Pasquale had to go through the Canadian consulate to get their visa, which wasn't a problem, and the wait wasn't nearly as long because they'd already been approved - as had the rest of us - when my father got his approval during our trips to Naples.

Just as when my father left, it was another happy and sad time, and just as when my father left, a car came to house to pick them up. It was a 1940s black taxi with a back seat and two lift up seats in the middle to sit two additional people. I was excited for any chance to see a fancy car, even if it was tempered by the fact that it meant that my older siblings were leaving.

It was hard to have another piece of our family leave us behind, but it also meant that we were another step closer to fulfilling our dream of being together in America. I already missed my father terribly, and was unsure if my heart could stand missing Anna and Pasquale as well, but I did my best to hang in there, knowing that one day I too would be in that car, making the three hour trip to the coast, and onward to America.

My siblings booked passage on the *Saturnia*, which disembarked in Halifax, Nova Scotia. Anna spent most of the journey seasick, but Pasquale was having the time of his life. He had never been on a boat that big before.

They were both a little shocked having left the beautiful Italian city of Naples only to arrive in the cold grey city of Halifax. They disembarked and were checked over to make sure that they didn't smuggle in anything illegal, before being herded onto a train to Toronto where they would meet up with our father and continue on to Sarnia.

While on the train, Pasquale experienced his first problems with the language barrier. The train had a lunch cart, but Pasquale couldn't speak English so he didn't know how to ask for anything. He wound up eating a lot of sardines, because he knew what the picture was and could point to it.

He didn't know how much the money was worth either and would simply hold out his hand and hope that the person taking it was honest. He soon learned that pennies weren't worth very much because no one ever took them. At first he was confused about the dime and nickel, because the dime was worth more but was smaller.

Before he learned English, the language barrier would almost prove deadly for Pasquale. One day soon after his arrival in Sarnia, he was running through the rain to catch a bus home. The storm had been building in intensity when suddenly a tornado touched down. He had never seen a tornado before, let alone know what one was and was terrified to see it the funnel heading towards town, ripping down buildings right in front of him.

He managed to catch the bus, but it was quickly evacuated right before the tornado caught up with it. He was confused as to what was happening as panicked people rushed past him and out into the street. Like most people, when he soon realized that everyone was running in the same direction, he followed suit.

Once again out in the street, he found himself bucking the heavy winds, and ducking the flying debris. He ran for shelter in a nearby bar, but they wanted him to leave because he was under age. Pasquale tried to explain the circumstances, and that he only wanted shelter, but stumbling over his words, he couldn't. He fought to stay as the tornado passed, but even after it did, he still had to walk another five miles in the rain just to get home.

After Pasquale and Anna left, life was harder on my mother. She was now alone with Ortensia and three young children - at the time we were nineteen, ten, eight and six - and also had to run the farm, and we still didn't have too much to go around.

As was the tradition, we fasted for the holidays, eating just a piece of bread and an onion, which made it easier on the food supply. We had a deep appreciation for everything we did and everything we got, and were always thankful to God for the things that we had.

With Pasquale gone, it was another male influence that had left the house. As I mentioned earlier, in the Italian household the male is considered to be the protector of the house and the family, and so despite my age, that role fell to me.

I was only eight years old when Pasquale left and my mother came to me and said, "Well son, you're the only male in the house. Naturally you have to listen to me, I am your mother and after all, you're only eight years old, but you are the man of the house and with that you have the responsibility to look out for your sisters and help out and look out for me and for the benefit of this family."

It was a different transition after Pasquale and Anna left, as now I had to be the head of the household and look out for everyone. I still had to do what my mother said, but I was the man in charge. I wondered how I would handle such a tremendous responsibility.

It helped that I was afforded the respect of a grownup by my sisters. I had to be on the lookout for whatever happened. The male position at that time in Italy was a protective role for the family. I always had to know where my sisters were. Still, it wasn't a position of power, but a position of responsibility and love for my family members.

My mother established the rule that if I said something even to my older sisters, they would need to listen and obey, but it was out of respect. I wasn't saying, "Now I'm the man of the house and I can do whatever I please." It wasn't that way at all.

To tell you the truth, at times I considered it more of a burden then a pleasure, but really it was both, and it gave me a huge sense of responsibility at a very young age. There were times when I felt powerless because I was so young and I couldn't do all that I wanted to do, but it was an honor to be respected in that fashion.

Even though my sisters agreed that I was the representative head of the household, there were times when it caused some friction, such as the next year at a festival held at my father's hometown of Sora.

We went to the huge feast that started the festival and were surrounded by a multitude of people. We had a great time at the morning mass and in the procession, followed by a delicious meal at a friend's house. In the evening, Ortensia went off with her older friends, while Concetta and Loreta left in a different direction with our younger friends.

I knew that it was my duty to watch out for all of them, so of course I had a dilemma. There was no way for me to be in two places at once, so I went back to talk to my mother and told her that I decided that it was time for us to leave and go home.

It's a huge festival, so there were a lot of people there - thousands of people. I told her that I couldn't look out for my sisters the way I wanted to look out for them because they both went off in different directions. My solution was simple nine year old logic - if I couldn't watch after everyone, then it was time for us to go home.

My mother looked at me and said, "You know if you feel that way, you're right, let's make arrangements to go home."

So my mother and I went and collected my sisters, none of whom were happy to hear the news - most of all Ortensia, who was twenty by that point. My sisters begrudgingly bid their friends farewell, and we went to leave.

In order for us to get home, however, we also had to disturb another young man's feast time because he had to drive us all the way back to Vicalvi. He was pretty ticked off at me, as to him I was just this young snot nosed kid who was overly insistent about protecting his sisters.

After loading us all into his Peugeot, he sped off towards home. I was sitting next to him in the front seat staring with wide-eyed panic at the speedometer as the needle inched more and more to the right, eventually getting all the way up to 115 km as he raced us home down the two lane road.

He took us back around nine o'clock at night, instead of well after midnight when the festival closed. Because of that none of us were able to enjoy the whole feast and missed the fireworks. My sisters weren't happy with me for a few days, but they soon got over it.

Being head of the household meant more than policing my sisters; mostly it meant learning to help others and be responsible, and learning it while very young. I really believe that in helping others you achieve your own success, so the more I help people, the more successful I feel.

After my brother left, the only machinery that we had on our farm was a donkey. That was the machinery for doing farm work. The horses were gone because those animals couldn't be taken care of by young children or by my mother alone, so we had to sell them and use our donkey for all the heavy work.

As the man of the house it was my duty to clean the barn and take the manure out to the fields. When it began to pile up, I would get up at sunrise, put two baskets, one on each side of our donkey and fill them up with manure. I'd take the donkey out into the fields, untie the ropes and carefully slide the baskets down his sides. It would usually take two trips to get all of the manure out to the fields.

When the town clock would ring at 8:15 in the morning, I would head back home, get cleaned up, and start the two kilometer trek up the mountain to school. At that age that was quite a journey and I'd have to rush and run uphill to make it on time. At least when I went home it was all down hill.

When school was over I would take my donkey, along with a couple of goats, out to the fields to graze. Every piece of land that could be used was used to grow crops, so I would take the animals to graze on the side of the road. It was terribly boring and lonesome out there alone with them, so to pass the time I would count the seconds to see how close I could come to the clock on the bell tower. It wasn't much of a game, but soon I could time it out to the very second.

Every Sunday, and during holidays, I'd cut some grass with the sickle and bundle it up, mix it with straw and feed the animals so that they wouldn't have to go on the roadway during the feasts on saint's days, or other religious occasions.

As I've said, our lives were pretty simple back then. Wake up, do your chores, back to bed - but behind it all was an incredible yearning for our reunion in America.

Chapter 7

As the days became months, and eventually years, we continued to ask our mother when we'd be rejoining our family in America. In fact, "When are we going?" was the most asked question in the house.

The waiting was unbearable, but my father wanted to wait until things were perfect before we came. He wanted a car for us to drive in, and a house for us to live in.

Every day I'd run out to the postman to see if he had any letters from my father or older siblings. My mother would take them and read them out loud to the four of us. The letters came on a weekly basis, but I always wanted more.

Over in Canada, my father had gotten Pasquale a job with him in construction. One of their first jobs together was helping to build a new hospital. Pasquale was only sixteen at the time and there was a big argument between the man who hired him and the Union rep. They said they couldn't pay him the minimum wage of $1.32 an hour and he would have to settle for $1.10 because of his age.

Pasquale didn't see what the problem was - in Italy he couldn't even make $1.10 in an entire day's worth of work.

Because of the low pay he was given extra hours. He worked ten hours a day, six days a week and because of it, he was soon taking home more than most of the Union workers.

In 1954 we got a letter from my father letting us know that Ortensia received approval to come join him. Having another family member leave was no easier to take that the previous two times, but it began to seem more and more likely that the rest of us would be making the journey at some point soon.

Ortensia was a seamstress and she was fantastic at it. In Italy, May is the month of the Madonna of the Rosary, and Catholics say the rosary every day. The May before she left, Ortensia volunteered our house to hold the Madonna, which goes from house to house during the month. Each home has an altar to keep her in, but Ortensia decked out our room for it. By the time she was done, it didn't look like a room anymore; it was covered in canopies with velour blankets on the walls.

That seemed like Ortensia's final gift to us and our town before she left Italy to join my father, Anna and Pasquale in Sarnia. Our friend Palmerino had a limo service and he came to pick her up and take her to the port. She left on one of the biggest, most luxurious ships at the time - the *Andrea Doria*, and she was on its penultimate voyage before it tragically sunk entering New York harbor.

In 1955 we received word that Anna was getting married to a man named Jerry Iadapaolo, a fellow immigrant originally from a bordering town near Vicalvi, who was living in Detroit. After her wedding she moved there, making her the first of our family to become a citizen of the United States. Naturally we all wanted to be together for such a blessed event, but were unable to. We were sent plenty of pictures, but all of us - my mother especially - wished we could be there.

In August of 1956 we finally got word that it was time for the rest of the family to come to America. There was lots of excitement - but we couldn't leave until November, because we needed to wait until after the next grape harvest and sell all of our animals before we left.

Those four months seemed to drag on endlessly, but I knew that when November came, I'd be starting my new life in America. We were filled with joy as we went about making our preparations and finalizing everything. A few weeks prior to our day of departure, we had completed all of the things that we needed to.

Because we were leaving in November, I still had to go to school in the fall, but my heart just wasn't in it. I got so bad that in the last few weeks before we left, I flat out simply didn't go. I didn't try and hide it either. I would walk around outside the school where the other kids could plainly see me.

Ultimately I was kind of bored because there was nothing for me to do when I wasn't going to school - not that I ever considered returning. The kids were all happy for me, though for some of them it was because they were waiting to see what I'd give them before I left.

Every so often as a kid I would get a mean streak in me. One of the girls at school promised me that she would buy my schoolbooks. I told her that she could buy them, but she had to pay me. Every day she said she'd bring the money, and every day she forgot. I insisted that I wouldn't give her my books until she paid me. Once November came around, everything I owned was packed except my books, which I left out for her.

Before bed one night, I waited at home with my other friends for her to come by and finally buy my books. Deep down I knew that she wasn't going show up. I remembered all of the people who owed my father money and knew that they were never going to pay him back. With this in mind, I defiantly grabbed my books and declared, "Tell Laura that her books got burned!" and promptly threw them in the fire. It wasn't one of my proudest moments, for certain.

I guess I got a little wild in those last few months. I couldn't contain the excitement that I was feeling, and the anticipation of not only finally being able to start my new life in America, but also finally getting to rejoin my family and see my father again was too much for me to take. I wanted to leave, and I wanted to do it immediately.

Chapter 8

In late November of '56 it was finally time for our journey to begin. Once again, our friend Palmerino came to pick us up and take us to Naples. We loaded up the car, and the majority of the townspeople came out to bid farewell to everybody. All the kids and all my childhood friends were there. Much like when my father left, it was another joyful, yet tearful goodbye.

As our car drove off, I looked back, saying goodbye to my old home, my old friends, my old life. Excitement filled me as we headed towards the port at Naples.

Once we arrived and unloaded I was able to look upon the ship that would take us to the New World - the *Vulcania*. It was enormous - like a multistory building, the biggest ship in the port. It filled me with pride to be boarding such a big ship.

Ready to embark for Canada, my family boarded the *Vulcania* under sunny Italian skies. It was a ten day trip starting in Naples, then to Genoa, Barcelona, Lisbon, and finally America. I watched from the rail as we pulled out and headed off, bidding good bye to my native Italy.

The *Vulcania* was an inconceivably big ship - bigger than then any ship I'd ever seen. It was all new and grandiose. The dining rooms had everything you could possibly imagine, and the ship was filled with luxuries. All of the men wore bow ties and smoked cigars. They spent most of their time drinking whisky and playing cards.

It was quite a sight going through Gibraltar. It was quite an experience to have it at an early age. Every time I saw those insurance commercials, I could relate to the rock. The Mediterranean may be huge, but as soon as we crossed the straight and hit the Atlantic, that's when it felt like we were really leaving.

I remember one gal on the ship was always dressed very prim and proper, and acted very sophisticated, but as soon as we hit the open ocean she became seasick and remained so for the rest of the trip. There was a lot of rough weather, so much so that they put out ropes for us to grab onto.

I was in heaven having the run of the ship. One day my sisters and I decided to head down to the engine room to see the turbines and shafts. Sneaking into the bowels of the ship, we were able to see the massive engines, with pistons as big as tree trunks. We would have loved to explore some more, but an engineer caught us and kicked us out.

Unlike in Italy, while we were on the ship we weren't allowed in the bar. At home children usually didn't drink wine, but could if they wanted, it was always available. When I was nine, my mom once joked, "You don't like wine - what kind of man are you?"

Here that kind of statement would be considered child abuse, but that's how the culture was in Italy and most of Europe. We never thought about getting drunk as teenagers because the alcohol was a part of everyday life - it just faded into the background and didn't matter.

To prevent seasickness while on the ship, my mother insisted that we wake up early every morning and never missed a meal. As we began to feel sick, the smell of food alone would make us feel queasy, but my mother insisted that we must eat. Besides, simply having three meals served to us every day was a welcome change. We also made sure to eat a lot of oranges and fruit to stay healthy.

Both of my sisters wound up getting a little sick anyway, and I knew that my mother wasn't feeling well either during the voyage, but she fought through it, and never admitted to us that she didn't feel well.

Our voyage held many unexpected surprises. As we were crossing the Atlantic a group of dolphins began following the ship. For me, a young boy of eleven, that was an incredible bonus - I'd never seen a live dolphin before, nor had I ever expected to see one.

The day before we reached our final destination of Halifax, Nova Scotia we also spotted a whale. Some of the older folks started to worry, as their only experience with whales came from Jonah's story in the Bible. The crew had to come and reassure them that everything was okay.

The next day I stood on the deck of the ship as it pulled into Halifax. It was December in Canada, so I don't have to tell you that it was cold. Bitter, frigid, cold. I had never felt anything like it - it cut right through you. I made sure to dress in layers, but it didn't matter, the frigid cold went right through my clothes.

We thought we had come prepared. We knew we were coming to a very cold country in the wintertime, but we had no idea how freezing it could get. Still, as jarring as it was leaving sunny Naples for ice cold Canada, the warmth of hugs from family members when we reunited would more than make up for it.

When the ship docked I could see a long red brick building with a rounded corrugated metal roof. Past that was a hill and on top were two dark log cabins. I had seen some cowboy and Indian movies as a kid and looking at my mother,

- with a tear in my eye - I said, "Ma - I want to go home." I thought that those two log cabins were where we were going to have to live.

After my mom reassured me, we left the ship and went through customs. Before we left Italy, my uncle told us that the customs agents looked like police because they wore uniforms, but not to be afraid of them.

That evening we boarded a train bound inland. As we headed for Toronto I began to absorb all I could about this new world that I had entered. I noticed that all of the houses were very short, because they were all little ranch houses and the snow was about halfway up the sides, and then there was another two feet of snow on the roofs.

A lot of the grown men that I was sitting near kept complaining about all of the snow, and complaining that all of the little houses looked like huts. I said that they were right, they did look funny, those little houses, but then I also pointed out that each house had a car parked out front! And that each house had an antenna - which meant they each had a TV too! I said that these people were living a good life. One of the grown men said to the others, "Look at that little kid, he's so observant!"

The new world suddenly started looking very, very good, even though it was buried in snow. It was easy to see that there was a better future ahead.

While on the train, we really didn't know how to order food, so my mother got us a loaf of bread, which we all shared. We'd never had American white bread before - it was like a sponge. Some of the grown women thought that it might be made from rice flour because it could be crumbled up into a little ball. All in all, no one was too happy with the white bread, but we loved being in our new country just the same.

As we went through Montreal, I was fascinated by the big lit up city - I'd never seen anything like it before. Only a few days in North America and I could already see that the stories that they told were true. Sure, there wasn't literally any gold flowing through the streets, but there may well have been.

All in all it took us four days to reach Sarnia from Halifax. In Italy the trains run very fast - after all, they do say that the one thing Mussolini did right was to make the trains run on time - but the Canadian train was stopped half the time. We joked that it was stopping for cars to go by.

Before we reached Sarnia we stopped off in Toronto, and there I received the greatest surprise of our trip - my father! I hadn't seen him in over five years! He looked tremendous - he was all dressed up, with a tie on and a long taupe trench coat and polished shoes. I was so excited I had to go to the bathroom - which, incidentally, led to my first English lesson.

My father gave me my lesson to save me from possible embarrassment. "Uomini" is the Italian word for "Men" and he wanted to make sure that I didn't go into the women's restrooms by accident, because "women" looks more similar to "uomini."

Once my father joined us, our trip to Sarnia went by in a flash. It was so wonderful being back with him. We continued on to Sarnia, and once we arrived I finally got to see my sisters and brother again, not to mention the newest addition to our family - my little niece Kathy, who was born before we came over.

The biggest shock was seeing Pasquale - he was a teenager when he left, but now he was almost twenty-one years old. I thought, "Oh my God - my brother is a man!" The young boy that I had remembered was gone. He could drive a car and everything!

Not only was there joy from our family finally being reunited, but we also knew that now our dream was coming true. My father had started to want to go to America since the end of the war eleven years earlier. It took more than a decade to get the whole family over and together again. It was unbelievable to actually be standing together with my family in America.

Once we arrived at our new home, I noticed that all of the houses looked a little different. My father took us for a tour and I saw that we had a basement. We didn't have basements in Italy! We had wine cellars, but certainly not basements.

In the basement was an oil furnace - I'd never seen one of those before. It was quite a luxury to have, though at night I thought that the sounds that it made were really monsters living in the basement. The oil furnace meant we had central heat! Heat in Italy was a fireplace.

Of course, it didn't get cold back in Italy like it did in here in Canada. It was so cold that before my father had bought our fridge he used to use the milk chute - the meat would freeze in there. I had never had a fridge before, or indoor plumbing, or anything that Americans consider standard living.

My father continued the tour of our new home. We found that every room was furnished - my mother was shocked.

"All the furniture!" she exclaimed, "You must be renting it and this must be costing a fortune."

He reassured her, "No, no, all the furniture is paid for." Then he added, "How do you like the house?"

This was a four bedroom house - kitchen, living room, and as I said, full basement, bathrooms, all that. The only thing she could think to say was, "You must be paying a fortune in rent for this house."

Incredulous, he said, "What do you mean paying rent?" Only then did he explain, "That's why it took me so many years to bring you and the rest of the family here, because I wasn't going to take you out of a house that we own in Italy and put you in a rented house here in a strange country. So this is your house."

Her jaw dropped before my mother threw her arms around him - hugging him and kissing him, with all the wait of five years of sacrifice and separation. Finally, we were home.

Chapter 9

So here I was in Canada. Now that our family was reunited, we were ready to take the next step and work towards our goal of living in the United States.

During our first day in Canada we had a lot of relatives come to visit us, along with many people who were sponsored or otherwise helped by my father to immigrate. To this day I have a lot of relatives in the United States and a lot more in Canada, and it's something that I'm very thankful for.

My Aunt Rosalba Petitta, my mother's oldest sister, had come over before the war had started, and lived in Pittsburgh. My mother always longed to see her sister again, and at the time they hadn't seen each other for almost 35 years. It was another of many, many happy reunions that day. We may have been in a new land, but it already felt like home.

We soon settled in and began to enjoy our new lives. The food was different, but that was a new experience to enjoy. Things were good and plentiful. We had meat every day, pasta every day - I was glad to find that the abundance that I had always heard about was true.

Not only did I luck out by coming to America, but I also lucked out because I got there in the first week of December, and because of the Christmas season, my parents, along with the principal of Our Lady of Mercy - the school that my sisters and I would be starting at - decided that it would be best for us not to start school until after New Year's.

Being eleven years old, I really felt doubly fortunate not having to go to school until the end of the year, which meant that I had a month or so with nothing to do. The only learning that I had to do was how to put on galoshes and get bundled up so that I could play outside in the snow.

I also soon learned something quintessentially American - how to watch TV everyday. In fact, I got pretty lazy for a while - I had no chores, no donkey, no goats or pigs or chickens, no manure to haul. I was living the good life. My first Christmas season in America was quite a festive one.

In Italy we celebrate Christmas, and it's a happy time, but it's really more of a religious celebration. I soon discovered the difference of the American Christmas celebration, and what eleven year old wouldn't love to celebrate Christmas in that fashion with all the lights and the presents and all of the things that go with it?

Of course all good things come to an end, and as 1957 began, my extended vacation was over and it was time to start school again. I had a ten minute walk to school, but by that point I was starting to adapt to the climate like everyone else. It was a chore getting unbundled at school with all those layers to take off.

I went to Catholic school and was taught by nuns. Because I didn't speak any English I was put a year behind the other kids my age and was also put in a special class where I learned to read English. I had a fun time there with the other immigrant children, sometimes laughing at someone else's pronunciation, sometimes at our own.

I was a good speller, and I taught myself how to pronounce English words using Italian phonetics. It helped me a lot, but didn't always work to my advantage. For instance, when I read about the French explorer Jacques Cartier I pronounced his name as: Jock-kwess Kar-tea-er. The other kids thought that was hilarious.

It's amazing to me that when I was growing up and going to school, I didn't know how to speak English at all. I also feel that I should point out that no one was forcing the school to hire teachers that could speak Italian to teach me. Underlying the process of my learning English was my strong desire to assimilate into my new culture - I wanted to be an American. I didn't want to say that I was different. The truth is, you should come to America to be an American. You come to America to enjoy America.

To be an American is not to say, "I'm different than you, and you have to bend over backwards to make me happy."

I never thought like that. My goal - my entire family's goal - was to be an American, and live like an American. We wanted to benefit from everything that America had to offer, and contribute everything that we could to our chosen homeland. That was, and always has been, my outlook.

Some people might have a different outlook, but in order to truly enjoy the American way of life, you have to become an American. To differentiate yourself is to disassociate yourself from your community. If the intent is to come to this country and enjoy the American way of life, then you don't want to create a different system. It's like marrying someone with the intent to change your spouse - it's not going to work. You should like the person for what they are.

In learning English and assimilating at twelve years old, I would open my mouth and say some things wrong, and that would make some people snicker. I don't know if I can attribute my desire to learn quickly to that, but it certainly didn't hurt.

Once my friend Nello Zeppa, who came over on the *Vulcania* as well, was supposed to read, "The mother was in the kitchen," but instead said, "The mother was in the chicken"

I raised my hand to correct him, but I was so excited that I had the right answer that I too yelled out "No, she was in the chicken!" The whole class - including the teacher - burst out laughing at that one.

Through-out my life, I've mostly been an introvert, and as an introvert I never pictured myself making a living in sales, and I never pictured myself doing a talk radio show on the weekends, but I do both.

When I was first learning English, however, I never spoke unless what I had to say was of important consequence, or meaning. Small talk was something that I could just never do. I refrained from asking questions or raising my hand all the way through school because I was afraid that I didn't quite talk right.

The hardest part of school wasn't the language barrier, however, rather it was the French Canadian boys - they didn't like anyone, especially immigrants. They started fights with the immigrant students constantly, and it got to the point where there wasn't even any communication - if you even looked at them the wrong way they would come at you, bodies tensed and ready to fight. They'd take any excuse to start throwing punches. It was almost daily that there was some sort of altercation.

At our Open House my teachers told my parents that I was a good kid while at school, but at recess I would always be caught fighting. However, my parents still didn't understand English very well, so I had to translate for them.

When my teachers told my parents that I was fighting too much, I told my parents that the teachers said that the French Canadian kids were picking on me, and forcing me to defend myself.

I thought I was pretty clever, but my teachers caught on to my ruse pretty quickly. The next week they called my parents back in and told them the same thing, - only this time they asked my brother to come in and translate for them instead.

Pasquale did, but when he got home he took me aside and said, "If you let anyone beat you up, when you get home I'll beat you up too."

It sounds harsh I know, but he understood that I was only being attacked because I was Italian and he wanted to make sure that I stood up for myself. In any case, things calmed down later in the year once I began understanding and speaking English better.

Within six months - just about to the end of the school year - I was able to speak English very well. I adapted very quickly and everything started to fall into place. The following summer I even made friends with some of the Canadian kids, and we spent most of our summertime exploring in the woods, playing Huck Finn.

Around the same time, because I was a minor and my father had already been in Canada for five years and was a Canadian citizen, I too officially became a citizen of Canada, along with the rest of my family.

Chapter 10

I would like to say that our first year in Canada was nothing but happy times, but unfortunately it will forever carry a dark mark for my family.

Out of all the children, my sister Ortensia was the sweetest one. Soon after we arrived in Canada she became engaged to Orfeo, a man from our hometown back in Italy.

One night my parents took Concetta and Loreta to visit with some friends a couple of blocks away. Pasquale was out as well, so I stayed home with Ortensia. I noticed that she seemed upset. She was on the phone all night and I thought that she might have been crying, but I didn't know, and didn't want to be rude and eavesdrop.

Around nine at night she told me that she was going to our neighbor's house, who was a fellow seamstress. When my parents and sisters came home they were curious as to where she was. When the clock hit eleven, she still wasn't home, which was very unusual.

I told my parents that she said she'd be at our neighbor's house, so they decided to head over, but when they arrived, the lights were off. They knocked on the door, but our neighbor said that Ortensia didn't come there all night.

My parents kept searching. Pasquale came home around 11:30 and began calling all over, but no one knew where she was. He called the police, but because she was over twenty-one, said that they couldn't do anything about it.

As the night wore on, the younger kids, myself included, were put to bed, but Pasquale and my parents continued to search. Finally around 8:30 in the morning, we got word that someone walking along the beach by Lake Huron found her. Found her body. She had drowned.

There was no foul play, and it soon became evident that she had taken her own life. We discovered that Orfeo was breaking off the engagement and was leaving her. Ortensia's tender heart couldn't take it, she simply couldn't cope.

I was the last one to see my sister alive. She left a letter behind explaining her reasons. Everyone else in the family has read the letter, but to this day I never have. I never even asked my parents about what it said - I just didn't want to bring it up again. To this day, I've never read the letter she left.

Needless to say, it was very rough on our family. It was even harder on my parents because the Catholic Church didn't want to perform the funeral rites for a suicide victim. My parents had to convince them that she didn't take her own life, but rather drowned because she couldn't swim.

In the end, the church relented and gave her full rites. Ortensia was such a warm person. She would do anything for people. She always helped, was always there, and touched so many people that not just the Italian community, but virtually the whole town of Sarnia showed up for the funeral. It was the longest funeral procession the city had ever had.

Every year those in my family who still live nearby have a Mass for her and my brother and sisters who live further away also visit her grave once or twice a year.

My family continued on past that dark period, pulling together all the more to gain a foothold in our new land. The whole family pitched in and got jobs to help out, hoping to save up enough for us to make our final move to the United States.

Because my father's English was limited, he worked as a laborer - helping to build refineries in Sarnia. My brother did the same thing, but because he could speak better was more of a superintendent, though later on he became a builder as well.

After she turned fourteen, Concetta started working as a nurse's aide at a hospital, and later became a pharmacist. Because we were too young, Loreta and I continued school, but when we got a little older, however, we too took jobs so that we could contribute and help out the family.

After I hit the eighth grade I started working at the local car wash. For three dollars a day I spent ten hours drying cars. My mother suffered more from seeing me work those hours than I did. I had a lot of energy and didn't mind doing it. In fact I quite enjoyed getting to inspect all of the different cars as I dried them off.

I worked so hard that I soon got promoted and started getting six bucks a day. Even at fourteen, however, I wanted something better than the car wash, so I eventually quit and began working as an usher at the Odeon Theatre.

I felt very proud to work as an usher because I got to wear a uniform and a hard shirt front with a tie and a jacket. It was a lot better than working at the car wash. I felt a lot more respectable - it's amazing what a uniform can do for you.

All of the money that my siblings and I made was pooled together. We would give all of our pay to my mother, and then she'd give us each an allowance. Mine was fifty cents; the rest of the money was for the good of the family.

This isn't to say that when we wanted to buy something bigger we couldn't, we only had to ask. My parents always expected us to work hard and pool our money with the family, but were always extremely fair in compensating any of us when we needed it.

I always felt that that was one of the reasons why all of us don't quibble about splitting things - who's getting more or less. It's very comforting to have siblings who just enjoy each other to the fullest.

While working at the theatre, I wanted to buy a bike so I wouldn't need to walk back and forth there every day. I asked my mom for $65 so that I could get a brand new bike and she gave it to me from the money that she had kept that I had already earned.

It was nice owning a bike so that I could ride it not only to work, but for the two mile trip to my junior high. That is, I was able to ride it for most of the year. Once winter came around however, there was so much snow on the ground that I had to walk again.

By the time I hit high school, my desire to move to the United States was still burning deeply. All of our TV channels were from Detroit and all of them were about America. Every day I watched and absorbed all I could, yearning for the day when we could move there.

Every weekend we'd go visit Anna and her husband in Detroit, and every weekend I'd ask my parents, "Why don't we move here?" I never liked it when we crossed the Bluewater Bridge to go back into Canada. I wanted to stay in the United States.

It's not that I didn't like Canada, but it just wasn't the United States. It wasn't the America that I wanted, that I still dreamed about living in.

Anna was eventually able to sponsor my father and the rest of our family to come over to the United States, and we once again had to go through the visa process again - get our physicals, visit the consulate, get our approvals and so on. It was a little easier this time, having gone through the process before, but the anticipation was still there - this time we were headed for the United States!

My father got all of our paperwork done, allowing us to leave Canada for the United States, and he moved to Detroit to set things up. Once again the rest of the family had to stay behind while he was preparing the next stage of our lives, but it wasn't nearly as bad as last time.

This time around we weren't separated by an ocean, just a lake. Sure it was a Great Lake, but we had a bridge. We could drive over and see him whenever we wanted. Still, I was filled with the same sense of anticipation. I needed to finish up school - I continued to go this time - and eight months later, the rest of our family made the move to Detroit. We arrived in the first week of July - just in time to celebrate our first Independence Day. A very exciting time to be an American!

Chapter 11

In July of 1962 I crossed the border to Port Huron. I was now an American. My father got us a home in Detroit, MI and moved the whole family over to the United States.

Unfortunately we still had one family member who hadn't quite fulfilled the dream of living in the US with us. By this point Pasquale was now a legal adult and a citizen of Canada, so he wasn't able to come with us to Detroit and instead moved to Windsor, Ontario. He would come to spend the weekends with us, but it took him another five years to get his visa and join us in America.

When my father sold our house in Canada he gave my brother a percentage of the profits, since he had used the money that my brother earned in order to help pay for it, and that in turn helped Pasquale to make a decent start.

Once in the United States, the biggest difference that I noticed between the US and Canada was the population size. Sarnia is a small town of less than 50,000 people; Detroit at the time had over three million. Of course my observation had more to do with where we moved to than any real difference between the two countries themselves, but my childhood vision of the grandiose United States came to a full realization - here we were in the Big City.

I had my first real experience with the vast diversity of America when I started school in the United States in September of 1962, attending Thomas M. Cooley High. In Canada I went to a private Catholic high school, but Cooley was a public high school. There I experienced a vast mixture of races and religions.

I always knew that the United States was a much more diverse place than Italy, but it wasn't until I started at Cooley that I got to experience the melting pot first hand. The school was also a lot more liberal in what students could do, and what they could wear. We didn't march single file to class any more, everyone was able to move independently. I can't think of a better metaphor for what it was like to now be in America.

There were other noticeable differences, too. Living in Canada in the late fifties and early sixties, I didn't really grasp what the controversy was during the rise of the Civil Rights movement.

While in Canada, I lived near a black family, though I never knew them, and when I grew up in Italy things were pretty homogeneous as well. I only saw a black person once before I came to America. When it came to people of a different color or race, I simply didn't see what all the hoopla was about.

Once my family and I moved to Detroit, I saw that there were some bad areas, and a lot more crime overall. Then I started to see why people saw differences, but still I didn't understand why people were calling it a racial issue.

Crime wasn't a racial issue, it was economic. It still is. To this day I still don't understand how race gets mixed in with the issue. Crime is worse in poorer areas - it doesn't matter what the racial mix is.

You simply can't put people into a group and say, "You're all like that." It's ridiculous. Nor should we want everyone in a group to be the same. We should celebrate our differences, not shy away from them, or try to be politically correct to avoid them. The strength of this country comes from its diversity. If no one was different we'd be in a bad place.

My father continued his work in construction, and in fact most of our relatives went into construction work as well because of the language constraints. In Canada, my cousin, who was younger (and therefore learned English a lot quicker) was elected president of the labor union after only five years on the job. The labor force continued to mostly be made up of Italian immigrants, and so he was able to hold his position for fifteen years.

Even though we were now in America, I continued to work to help contribute to my family. I started working in the men's department at JC Penney's in the spring after we moved and continued there until I graduated in 1964.

After my graduation from high school, I began attending Schoolcraft Community College. Being an immigrant, you don't come to this country with a suitcase full of money - maybe some people do, but not my family. All we had in our suitcases were clothes, and maybe if we were lucky, a second pair of shoes.

So we all had to work hard, and I didn't really have the money to go to school, but I had parents that were supporting me, and were behind me and wanted me to get an education. Because I was working at the same time that I was going to school, and I only had to pay six dollars per credit hour, I was able to afford my education.

I registered at Schoolcraft the first year it opened, and was one of the school's first students. My fellow students and I became a very close knit group because of that. My sophomore year my friends and I started a soccer team, I was co-captain of the team along with my friend Olindo.

In 1965 my parents moved to East Detroit City, and I transferred to Macomb Community College. I started a soccer team there as well and was a full fledged coach and captain. We wound up playing the team that I had started over at Schoolcraft and ended up with a 500 season, though we only played five games.

I went to school envisioning a career as an engineer, but after three semesters, I realized that calculus and some of the other higher math courses were not really suited for me, or rather, I wasn't suited for them.

Once I decided to change majors, I started thinking about transferring to the University of Detroit which at that time was $18 per credit hour. By today's standards that's very inexpensive, however that was three times what I was paying per credit hour at community college. I talked to my counselor and found that most of the credits that I had already earned could apply to Business Administration at the University, so I switched my majors.

Because of the added expense, I began looking for a more lucrative job and was soon hired by Stouffer's Restaurants, where, even though I had yet to turn twenty-one, I trained to become a bartender. Once my training was complete, I left Stouffer's and went to work at a private restaurant, The Kolping, tending bar.

At The Kolping there was a regular who used to come in, smoke a cigar, and have a few drinks, all while looking and studying maps. One night he left everything sitting at the table and went to get some fresh air.

When he saw me standing by the doorway making sure that he wasn't going to run out on the bill, he laughed and said that I was a sharp guy. He introduced himself as Sam and immediately offered me a job as manager of his coffee shop which was combined with a double lane car wash.

Sam turned out to be a well connected little Sicilian gentleman. He had his car wash and coffee shop and was a partner in a night club, in a dairy, in a hotel, and did a lot of gambling on the side. I soon became one of his most trusted employees and had the run of his office and his whole operation. Some days I just sat around and waited for someone to come by with an envelope for him. I'd take it and put in the safe - no questions asked.

He soon invited me to meetings with his partners where they would discuss which judges to support and donate money to, and politicians, and general business info that was over my head. He even gave me his big Cadillac to drive on the weekends. Everybody knew that I worked for Sam and when I went to the bar I didn't wait in line.

My life as a big shot wound up being short lived - maybe for the better. When I changed majors, some of the credits that I had earned didn't apply to my new major in Business Administration. So at the end of my two years, because I changed majors, I could still take courses at Macomb Community College that I could transfer to the University of Detroit, and I could still continue paying six dollars per credit hour instead of eighteen.

Naturally, I took the less expensive route and registered a fifth semester at Macomb for my studies. What I didn't know was that by doing so it meant that I was going to lose my deferment for the draft.

I hadn't been in the United States for five years, so I was still a legal alien. At that time, legal alien was a status and you were a permanent resident who had to report every year. Everything was systematic and there was no blatant flaunting of the laws by illegal aliens like today. It was something to behold to be given the opportunity to come to this country; we wouldn't dare to take advantage of it.

I was now living, working, and going to school in the United States, and I wanted to spend the rest of my life here, but at this point I was still a Canadian citizen. However, if you were a legal permanent resident in the United States you could be drafted, you did not have to be a citizen.

This was in 1966, during the height of the Vietnam War and soon after I lost my college deferment, I got my notice to report for the draft. After I received my draft notice, Sam reassured me that when I came home I would have a job waiting for me. He said that he'd make sure that I'd pick up right where I left off. He then slipped me a few bills and wished me well. Ultimately, having grown a little wiser, I didn't take him up on his offer, which I'm positive was for the best.

Chapter 12

No sooner had I received my draft notice, all of my relatives in Canada began telling me that I should come back over the border instead of joining the military. After all, I was still a Canadian citizen, and there were a lot of American born citizens who protested the war and were sneaking into Canada to avoid the draft.

I had fifteen or so cousins in Sarnia, Windsor, and Toronto, all of whom urged me to cross back over. They would say, "You're a Canadian citizen. Come on back. If born Americans are fleeing the country illegally, why shouldn't you if you can do it legally?"

They were right. I could have easily run back home - I only lived about fifteen minutes from Windsor, Ontario. I could've gotten there by bridge or tunnel, but I didn't think it was right.

Whether they said it or not, no one in my family wanted me to have to go into the Army during the Vietnam War, but I insisted that I do my duty and I felt that I would have been a hypocrite if I went back to Canada now after so many years of hardship trying to become an American. I wanted to be in this country for the rest of my life, so how could I leave right when my country needed me?

When he was a young man, my father migrated to France. He was living there when he got his draft notice for the Italian Army. He could've stayed in France, but he chose to do his duty and leave France for his military service in Italy.

Having served during the Second World War, my father never pushed me one way or the other. Rather, he wanted me to make my own decision before letting me know where he stood. Not everyone in my family took that route, however. Loreta for one, tried really hard to stop me from going into the service. She pleaded with me to find a way to either go back to Canada or not go into the military. She kept at it right up until the last day, when she drove me to Ft. Wayne in Detroit to report for duty. Even as I stepped out of the car she pleaded with me not to go and to let her drive me to Canada instead.

So I did my duty and went and got my physical and shortly thereafter got my greetings notice that I was going to be inducted into the service of the Army in the spring. Because of this my school career had to be put on hold and I didn't register for a semester in January.

Before I left I was given several kinds of advice, most of which centered around the fact that if I deliberately did poorly during my tests then they wouldn't want to put me in the tough jobs, and I just might stay out of harm's way.

I thought that it would be just as hypocritical for me to join up and then purposefully fail as to not go at all. When I took the tests - aptitude tests, IQ tests, not to mention all kinds of physical tests - I did them to the best of my ability and I still think that's the best thing to do. I didn't play dumb, and as it turns out, the Military wanted me to enroll in officer candidate school, but I had to turn it down.

I couldn't go to officer candidate school because that meant I would have to become a citizen. It was something that I had always wanted, but before I left, my father wanted me to promise that I wouldn't.

I said, "What do you mean? Of course I want to become a citizen."

He said, "Well I don't want you to become a citizen while you're in the Army."

And I said, "Okay, I promise but now tell me why," I didn't understand why he'd want me to promise not to do something that I'd been waiting for for my entire life.

His answer was, "Are you going to college to become a donkey?"

You see, in Italian when somebody asks, "Do you want to be a donkey?" that means, "Do you want to just be a dumb animal?"

I said, "Why do you say that?"

He told me, "The United States has not declared war on Vietnam, so this is an undeclared war. You are a legal alien, a permanent resident, but because it's not a declared war, the Army can't give you individual orders to go to Vietnam. The only way they can send you is to send the whole company over to Vietnam, so there's a better chance that you won't have to go overseas."

He said, "You can become a citizen the day after you come out of the service."

So I promised him, but at the same time, I had the opportunity to serve the country that I loved. After they processed my papers, they did a background check and then they gave me my secret clearance and sent me to Fort Knox for boot camp.

Everything you've seen in the movies about boot camp is exactly the way it was in real life. The best way I can think to describe it is that they break you down so that they can rebuild you the way they want, as a better person. A lot of personal dignity was put aside and you became one of the masses. You only spoke when spoken to, and you had to obey all of the rules. I went into basic training with the mindset of, "I'm here I'm going to do the best that I can." In the end I think that attitude served me well.

Following orders made life a lot easier then trying to buck the system. I was already older then most of the other draftees, and I used my knowledge and diplomacy to my advantage. They were always asking us to volunteer for different things, but the only thing that I ever volunteered for was to get my military drivers license.

Doing so meant that, instead of having to walk from one side of the fort to the other, I got to drive in the ambulance. In a couple of weeks the Drill Sergeant made me a squad leader, so I had that responsibility. I had to lead the other solders in the march, so I had to march a little bit as well but I still drove whenever I could.

Maybe it's because I'm Italian, but I was never happy with the food we were given in boot camp. The only time that I had previously seen grits was when we fed it as slop to the hogs, but now it was on my dish in front of me every day. I never did acquire a taste for it. My appetite, however, was enormous, so no matter what I had in my tray, I always cleaned my plate.

We had exercise in the morning, exercise in the afternoon, and exercise at night to build up a strong physique. By the time I was done I had a thirty inch waist and weighted 165 lbs. Ultimately it was a good experience, though of course I missed my family tremendously. The hardest time about boot camp was the two week delay in getting orders for my next assignment. That was due to not being a citizen.

It was a good thing that my father warned me that the military would try and trick me, because he was right. After I left Fort Knox I was stationed in Fort Gordon, Georgia, in Military Police School. While I was there, they wanted me to sign citizenship papers without telling me what they were. Luckily, I discovered what the ruse was and I didn't sign them.

Ninety seven percent of my company got orders to go to Vietnam, but because I didn't sign, I couldn't go and was one of the few that received orders to go to Ft. Myers in Arlington, Virginia. There, for almost eighteen months, I had the pleasure of being stationed right next to Washington National Cemetery.

One of my most memorable duties - as minor as it may seem - was the duty at five o'clock to take down the American flag at Ft. Myers. Cannons boomed as we folded the flag in perfect military fashion, with all the pomp and ceremony. The field that the flag was flown at was surrounded by the General's quarters.

I was also sent to pickup documents from the Pentagon and take them to other military and government establishments around DC, which allowed me to visit all the historical buildings around the city. It was really awe inspiring.

Being an immigrant, every so often, as I drove past certain landmarks I would misspeak one of the famous names, which my fellow soldiers found quite amusing. Once while driving along the Potomac, I said to the other three soldiers in the car with me, "So this is the famous Poe-toe-mack River." They found that quite funny. It was just like being back in Junior High.

I was also assigned to guard the gravesite of the late president Kennedy during war demonstrations. Like most Americans who were alive at the time, I too remember exactly where I was when President Kennedy was assassinated.

My friend Olindo called me, and told me that President Kennedy had just been shot. I didn't believe it until I turned on the TV. My mother was in tears. We had only been in the US a short time, but we all felt that he was our president and a good man.

Another one of my duties was to make regular patrols around the Iwo Jima Memorial to prevent protestors from messing with it. Ft Myers is split into North Post and South

Post, where the Pentagon is, with Arlington in the middle. Whenever we went from North Post to South we'd drive over the bridge, right by the Lincoln Memorial, so I always had it in my sight. It was a really awesome experience, because this was the heart of America and I was in the center of it.

During my off duty hours, I worked at the Ft. Myers Officer's Club as a bartender. I was very much a Democrat, so when Nixon was elected, I told everyone who I served that they better hold on to everything, cause things were going to get tight. Even so, I was honored when I was asked to work behind the scenes at Nixon's inauguration. I even have, to this day, a certificate of appreciation for doing so.

Taking my own economic advice, I saved up enough money to buy a car and I split the rent of an apartment with three other soldiers, so that really helped me make ends meet, and I always had people to hang out with at night.

I always found it interesting that when the four of us went out at night and weren't wearing our uniforms, the Hippies and soldiers would party together, but when we were stationed on the inside of the fence at the Pentagon, we'd be busy dodging the spit that these same people hurled our way. They may have wanted peace, but they didn't have much respect for us.

Having to deal with the protesters and the rioters are why even though I was stationed domestically, I still say that I had to defend my country. Riots that were happening all over Washington at the time and my conflicts during the Vietnam War were with the demonstrators who were protesting against the war not only at the Pentagon, but at other various sites around DC.

As an Armed Forces policeman, I was really in the middle of it all. I was assigned to escort columns of soldiers and National Guardsmen from the Pentagon to the parts of the city that had erupted in violence.

During one riot I had to take a convoy of two and a half ton trucks down the narrow streets of DC. Buildings were burning all around us, and the sweltering heat filled the streets.

The firemen had their hoses out to quell the flames and they wouldn't let me drive the trucks over the fire hoses which were crossed in the middle of the street.

The fire chief was making the whole convoy back up, and I had my superior, Colonel Gumf, arguing with me and telling me that I should go ahead and lead the convoy forward. It wasn't a pleasant argument, as I was a sergeant and he was a colonel, but I reminded him that my commanding officer was a two star general. So he finally relented and we left to find another route

During most of the riots we had to jump right into the fray. Storefronts were smashed in and buildings set on fire. It was hot and chaotic, but we had to try and calm the citizens who were tearing through the streets and senselessly destroying their own neighborhoods. It was hard to weed through and find the ones who were instigating and causing the most destruction, but we had to do all we could to protect the streets.

Compared to what everybody else had to go through overseas at the time, what I had to do was nothing, but even domestically things could get violent. We were so hated that at times during my patrols I would hear the "pop-pop" of gunfire as people shot at my car.

Sadly, shooting took place a lot during the riots. Looting was happening all over, TVs and appliances of all types were stolen, all the liquor stores were broken into and there was plenty of destruction all around. We'd wind up confiscating lots of guns, usually along with lots of whiskey.

It was a shame too, as these people were really only ruining their own neighborhoods. As always, while there were plenty of people who were following their hearts and doing what they felt was right in a peaceful way, many, many others were using the disruptions as an excuse to take what they could get for themselves, which naturally only made things worse for everybody.

Chapter 13

History proves, as always, that those who thought that they were right at the time still think they were right. Both the protesters and the soldiers thought that they were right in defending the country, and each in their own way.

The protesters believed that their honor and courage was in protesting against a war that they didn't believe in, but I feel that because of them we not only had an enemy abroad but we wound up with another enemy here inside our own country.

I think that those efforts were misguided, and instead of helping the United States win the war, it only helped the United States to come away a loser. I still feel that the war effort was compromised by the politicians, and as they say, history has a tendency to repeat itself and there's some forces at bay right now that almost seem to wish the United States to come to the same end.

The news media is dominated by extremists, mostly ultraliberal. They selfishly follow only their own personal politics and not what's best for the American people. In the ultimate end it really serves no purpose.

I fail to understand the extremist views - it seems that they have a death wish for this country. They seem to be so wrapped up in their own selfish viewpoints and they seem to have a real a hate for this country. They make it seem like the United States is the evildoer when it is not.

America is a very generous country, despite what all the criticism may have you believe. I really don't understand why the mainstream media is so critical of the United States. It's always looking to pin the blame on this country instead of being fair and calling the shots the way it should be called. I fail to understand that.

Our celebrities are just as bad. What makes our actors and actresses knowledgeable about anything? I mean some of them might be, but I don't think that Sean Penn, or Alec Baldwin or Susan Sarandon - I can name a lot more of them - are important statespeople who know the world and the laws, and the politics?

So you're a movie star. God bless you - you're a great movie star. That doesn't make you a great statesperson. But yet, because of their status they go on to criticize our country, and because of their status, people listen. Why?

Don't get me wrong, I believe that if there is any criticism to be put out there and it's truthful, then I have no qualms with that, but to base it strictly on a gut feeling or political leaning - that's not being truthful, it's being manipulative.

I remember as a child that the media always said good things about America. Can you imagine during World War II, the media giving or saying anything that would give the opposing forces some information that they could use to gain an upper hand?

But now, even the way that the news is reported, it's always filtered through an agenda. There are two ways to ask a question - one is to solicit a truthful answer, the other is to solicit the answer that you want. I think that the news is reported the second way.

Today the media, the way they report things, it's almost as if they hate America. They act as if they're not there to report the news, but they want to make the news. They are so full of themselves that at times they want to say things so that they'll shock the world, and they do. They try to draw attention to themselves, but in a negative way, not a positive one. Sometimes I think that the media is almost happy to report disaster.

I think the media has its own - and I don't want to get political, but they have their own political slants and they should be cognizant of that and then try not to sway people's beliefs.

If you want to report that the weather is bad, it shouldn't have any political side to it and if something is happening in government, then there shouldn't be any political side to it either. Whatever is happening around the world should not be reported based on a political agenda and when the news media starts to put a political spin on things, that's where they go wrong. They're not serving the country. They're just out to get ratings. That's not right.

We need to remember that the United States takes a lot of pride in fighting to help others and those that are oppressed around the world. My own life is proof of that.

Of course there's always somebody who disagrees. During the time when I was stationed in Washington, DC, I took incredible pride in what I was doing and I never regret having served this country at a time when there was a lot of discourse. There were those who believed that the war effort was right and those who believed that it wasn't right, but the one thing that no one appreciated at the time was that our soldiers were doing their duty to their country.

They were maligned and looked down upon instead of being supported like they should've been. The sacrifices and hardships that they had to endure were ignored. Not only that, but unlike today's volunteer army, because of the draft, many of them - myself included - didn't even choose to enter the service.

What the protesters didn't realize at that time was that what those soldiers were really doing was fighting for them and their right to demonstrate. Certainly they weren't fighting for the right to get spat upon when they came back home, but nonetheless that's what happened.

Its history, it's done, and we're fortunate to have moved on beyond that so that we realize today that our soldiers are looking to protect this country from terrorism, even if we as a nation can't always decide what the best course of action is to do so.

It may seem like once again our country is in a dark place, but this too shall pass and again this country will survive because it is strong and it is right in its beliefs and it is right in its Constitution. It was right when it was formed and it is right to defend it.

Mark Twain once defined a patriot as someone who "loves his country always and his government when they deserve it." I don't think anyone could sum it up any better. The country is the people and the politicians are meant to serve them. If what the government is doing is wrong, you need to call them on it - but always in an honest spirit. Politicizing the issues only serves the narrow needs of the party, and not the citizens of this country.

America is the best, but if we want to keep what we have, then we have to be willing to defend it because there are forces that are trying to destroy it. Whether we understand that or not, we have to look deep at what the goal of the enemy is. It doesn't matter who the president is, the country should be supported - whether that means supporting a president you agree with, or protesting one that you don't, you need to have the good of this country in mind.

Iraq for instance - the rhetoric is wrong. Is Bush wrong? Is Congress wrong? The real question is is the country wrong? In my heart, you cannot be a true American, and not support the country. To me, going against what the country is trying to achieve is going against your family. And you know we may differ politically, we may differ in all kinds of ways, but you know what it comes down to is deciding whether you're for the United States, or if are you for the opposing force. There should be no question. There should be no decision to be made - it's automatic.

We can talk about differences of political philosophies, but that's not what I'm about. I'm about this country being a great country. It has given me so much, it has given everyone so much. You really have to look back and ask yourself, "If I wasn't born here in this country would I be better off?"

It's our country and if we love it, we must defend it. If we believe in our rights, and we truly want to enjoy them, then it is our obligation to defend those rights so that they're not destroyed by others, both in the country or out.

What I really learned from my military experience was that if we reflect on and are thankful for what we have, then we're more apt to give something back and help others along the way. One of the things that I believe is that in life, the things you are blessed with, the good things that are done for you, you should repay. Even after only being in the United States for a few years, I was glad that I could serve it.

The most important part about my service is that it really made me feel like a citizen. To me, being a citizen means taking responsibility. Even if you don't break the laws, you may be a good person, but a good citizen is one who takes the responsibility to understand the system. If you're not doing anything to enhance your community and your country, then you might be a good person, but I don't think you're a good citizen. That's my interpretation, anyway.

In Washington, it saddens me to say, I don't think that we have a lot of patriots. What we have is a lot of politicians.

What is the difference between a politician and a patriot? Well the difference is that a politician serves for his or her own benefit. A politician says that they are going to serve for the people but ultimately their actions are based around the question, "How do I gain more votes so that I can get reelected?"

A politician is someone who forgets that his or her purpose is to serve the people and instead starts serving for his or her own benefit. Their rhetoric might be very inspiring during election season, but ultimately their actions are very self-serving and they serve really for their own benefit within the long run. That's a politician.

A politician does whatever they can to get reelected. A politician tries to get some pork to bring back home - not for the benefit of the American people, but for, say building a bridge that goes nowhere, just to create jobs in their home state so that their constituents will vote for them again so they can keep their job in politics. That's a politician.

What makes someone a patriot? It's certainly not someone who doesn't vote. You can't say, "Oh I just love my country, but you know my vote won't count, it won't make a difference."

Just one vote makes a BIG difference. Not every vote will be the tie breaker, but every vote counts the same - your vote, my vote, the President's vote. Being a voter, participating in the democratic process, that's part of my definition of a true patriot.

A true patriot is a person who puts their personal benefit aside and looks out for the benefit of the country. They respect the laws and at times does things not for their own good, but for the good of all, for the good of the country.

A patriot is one who works for the benefit of the country. They aren't self-serving, instead they serve the country, serve the office, and serve those who elected them. To me, that is the main difference.

A politician asks, "Is my action going to cost me votes?"

A patriot is going to say, "Are my actions right, and honorable and just and good for the country?"

The politician says, "I want go to Washington and I look for ways to stay there."

The patriot says, "I want go to Washington and serve the people and do what is best for them.

Sure, a patriot wants get reelected, but they don't do things just to get reelected, as a politician would. A patriot doesn't look at how their votes affect them personally. A patriot looks out for the benefit of their country. A politician looks out for the benefit of his wallet. To me that's the main difference between a politician and a patriot.

Chapter 14

The day I got my draft notice wasn't the best news that I received at the time. It caused a lot of controversy, and my family feared for my safety, but in the end things turned out just fine.

After two years, my service was over and I was honorably discharged. It was April 16th - I was let out a day early so that I would still be in the Reserves, which was common practice at the time.

Ultimately, my service in Washington was really rather pleasant. It was safer than being in Vietnam, that's for sure. I fulfilled my duty with pleasure and I'm extremely proud of the fact that I did what I could do for this country. After all it's done everything for me, so why not give a little bit back?

And how lucky can an immigrant be to be inducted into the military and then stationed in Washington DC - the seat of liberty, the capital of democracy? It was a huge honor to be able to work in the nation's capital.

After being discharged from the Army, I moved back home to Detroit to live with my parents. At that point, my brother and all my sisters were married, so I was the only one at home with them.

While I was gone, a lot had changed in the city. Several areas were completely destroyed from all the rioting. It was disheartening to see that the heart and soul of Detroit had been burned. Detroit was at one time the jewel of mid-west, but now had been reduced to rubble.

The change in the general attitude of the young people was what I noticed most. It was almost a free for all. It was now okay to smoke pot, be free sexually, to indulge in all the pleasures in life without any personal responsibility. None of it was for the betterment of society. A lot of rules had broken down, and it's affecting us as a society even today.

When I came out of the service, I began working in construction. I'd like to say that I did so because it would help rebuild the city that had become my adopted home. While that's certainly true, and I'm glad that my work had many positive effects in the community, by that point construction had become a family business.

As I've said before, when you come into this country you don't come over here a rich man. My father, even though he was a self-made businessman and landowner in Italy, had to go back to being a common laborer again when he came to this country because of the language constraints.

When my family came to the United States we all knew that opportunities were everywhere. My whole family was filled with entrepreneurial spirit and so after Pasquale followed my father into construction, he started his own construction company, partnering with my brother-in-law, Antonio Angeloni. I had already worked on construction jobs while I was going to college, so I joined them and began building.

I started out as an employee of their company, which was a member of the Garage Cement Contractor's Association. One day in the fall of 1969 Pasquale came to me and said that he had nominated me to be the President of the Cement

Contractor's Association for the Detroit Metro Area. I was both shocked and honored.

At the age of only twenty-four, I was running against three other candidates, all of whom were in their forties. Fortunately, by that point I was able to communicate in both English and Italian. There were a lot of Italians in the construction trade, so I'm sure that helped me out.

I waited patiently for the election results, not really expecting to win - in fact I hadn't even gotten over the fact that I'd been nominated at all. Once the votes came in and were tallied I was shocked to learn that I had won!

In January of 1970 I started my two year term as president. Being involved in the democratic process of election at only twenty-four and getting elected over men in their mid-forties really said to me, "Here's the American Dream." I was getting paid $16,000 a year, plus auto insurance, and more importantly, I was also getting a lot of respect.

As President, I got a lot of exposure to how a business is run and how to negotiate properly. My duties as President were to negotiate contracts between the subcontractors and the builders or suppliers. That's really where I honed the negotiation skills that I now use almost every day in my current line of work.

Everyone who I had to negotiate with was far older than I was, but I tried not to let that intimidate me. The youngest contractor that I dealt with was in his early thirties, but most of them were in their fifties and sixties. These were seasoned businessman - it was really something to go up against them and hold my own.

My secret to good business, and good negotiation was simple. I've mentioned a few times now that my family and I are very, very close, and that we always do our best to help each other out. I've always felt that if you maintain a good rapport with your family, it extends outside and it continues into the wider world.

If you take a family member's feelings into consideration, and you respect and hold it dear, then those same ways will carry over to your employees, business acquaintances and your life in general. If you lose that family connection, if you don't care about your own, then who do you care about? Things can fall apart very rapidly.

Negotiations may have been tough at times, but I was always honest. If there's any business advice that I'd give to anyone, it's that honesty is the best policy. It may be clichéd, but there's good reason for that. People who bottom line everything, and will do anything to get what they want really only create hollow victories for themselves. Taking advantage of everyone may get you what you want short-term, but in the big picture all you're doing is burning bridges to the future.

If you do something with honesty, you succeed, even if you fail, because it was an honest try. You can't build anything by stepping on the backs of others, but you can certainly build a lot of good businesses and organizations with the help of other people. It's the simple things that you do - and do right - that will take you furthest.

Even though I was young and inexperienced, I really held my own and began to make my mark in the world. I initiated education programs and had many of my GCCA members licensed as contractors and builders. The insurance that I negotiated is still with those members to this day and I was even interviewed by the Wall Street Journal, who wanted to know about the future of garage sizes, because cars - those huge boats of the seventies - were getting bigger.

It may not sound like much, but to me it was very significant. As an immigrant, I was fortunate just to come here, and now I had earned the respect of much older individuals, and my opinions were being solicited by one of the most respected business papers in the world. It was a very awesome feeling to have at the time.

All that said, as honorable and respectable as it was being President at such a young age. I was only in my mid-twenties and I felt that I needed more of a challenge, so instead of running for the position again I obtained my General Contractor's License and started building homes with my brother and brother-in-law.

Chapter 15

In the summer of 1972 while I was working as a contractor, a friend of mine began managing Anthony House, which at the time was one of the hottest nightclubs in Detroit. That fall, when it became much to cold to work construction, he needed an assistant manager and offered me the position, which I gladly accepted.

The club was frequented by both famous and infamous types. I remember one time when both the Detroit Lions and the Detroit Tigers were in the club at the same time and got into a scuffle. Other times there were mafia types who would come in and only occupy a certain corner of the bar and those who unknowingly ventured into that area soon found out that they weren't welcome. But there was never really any trouble there and for the most part it was a very enjoyable business-type establishment.

There was always a line of people waiting to get in at the door. As the assistant manager one of my jobs was to stand by the door and motion for the favorites to go around back and come in through the kitchen. After all, we couldn't keep Alex

Karis of the Lions or Billy Martin from the Tigers waiting in line.

One busy night I saw my friend Grace Licavoli standing in line with a friend of hers who I found absolutely stunning. I said hello to Grace and let her and her friend right inside. I told them to go into the dining room past the lobby, and it was there where Grace introduced me to her friend Patti.

The way that she was looking at me, I knew that she felt the same connection that I did. Shortly thereafter I went to their table and made some small talk - which as you know by now, was not an easy thing for me.

I bought Patti and Grace a drink and asked Patti if she wanted to meet me after I got off work and go have breakfast. She asked me what time I got off and I told her that bar closed at two in the morning and she said that that was out of the question for two reasons:

"One," she said, "I have to be home by midnight, and two, if you want to go out with me then you have to make a proper date and pick me up at my house."

I liked her approach and felt up to the challenge so I proceeded to get her phone number and the next day I called her for a date.

When I went to pick her up, naturally she was not ready (I think by design) so this gave her father a chance to give me a full interview. I was introduced to her parents, Luigi and Rose Badalamente. What struck me about them was what a young and beautiful couple they were. They had a well decorated home in a good neighborhood and I remember sitting there feeling like I was on 20/20.

By the time I left the house with Patti, Luigi knew everything about me, my family, Pasquale and Antonio's business, how much they grossed yearly, how much they took home and what my outlook was, my goals in life, and would I be interested in being a land developer.

Patti finally appeared, even more radiant than the first time that I saw her. As we left the house and the door closed behind us, she told me that she heard her father exclaim, "My son has arrived."

I took that to be a good sign that I was accepted by her family. Since she's an only child she was special to her parents and soon became very special to me.

Our courtship was short and sweet. I knew from the day that I met her that there was something more and I fell in love with her rather quickly. Within days of having met Patti, I knew that I wanted to marry her and within a month of our first meeting, I proposed to her.

As nervous or as intimidating as it may have been for me to propose, it was a lot more intimidating to ask her parents for her hand in marriage. Both requests were met with a positive response and we soon prepared for the wedding.

Patti's father owned a large restaurant and it had a huge banquet hall downstairs, so we planned our wedding at his restaurant. He said to me, "You can have a wedding elsewhere and it can be alright, or you can have a wedding at our place and everything will be extraordinary."

And it was. There were flowing platters of jumbo shrimp for appetizers, and filet mignon, lobster tails, and unlimited other dishes for dinner with an open bar, live music and around four hundred guests. As you can tell, it was a fabulous wedding.

During that time that we were engaged, our families got to know one another very well and we found that our backgrounds melded together very easily. Patti's father and brothers had fifteen hundred acres in Orlando that they were developing, and since I was in construction I decided to take a trip to see what was going on down there.

I left Detroit on a dreary January day, with not a green leaf in sight. I remember to this day as the jet took off all I could see was snow, barren trees and grey skies. As we approached

Orlando I saw paradise. The landscape was green and lush, dotted with lakes and before the wheels hit the runway I had decided that I was going to move to Orlando.

As the doors of the airplane flung open, I could feel the warmth of the Florida sunshine. It was the most welcoming warmth that I'd felt in years. Of course it reminded me of the Italian sun and the warmth that I'd known as a child. Not only was there warmth but there were palm trees and oranges and all of the things that I had seen during my childhood in Italy and hadn't seen since.

As I enjoyed seeing the sights of Orlando and its surroundings, I also noticed that there was a happier and friendlier attitude in the people. Maybe it's the climate, or maybe it's the palm trees, but Orlando seems like paradise, and I guess that's why people treat it as such.

My first visit to Orlando was about a month and half before we got married. While I was down there I rented an apartment. We got married on February 24th and by the 28th we had moved there. The Monday after we were married we loaded up a large truck with all our belongings, hitched the car behind it and drove together down to Florida.

We still had a ton of food left over from our wedding feast, and so I enjoyed having lobster tails during the drive down. I even put the butter on the truck's heater, so I had lobster dipped in warm butter, while sitting next to my new bride while I drove. All I could think at the time was that my life is series of dreams come true.

Chapter 16

It seemed like a good idea to move our construction company down to Florida. Winters in Detroit were harsh, and construction came to a standstill during winter because it was too cold to work until around March, so we'd lose a lot of money during those months.

I also relished the opportunity to move to a more favorable climate. I never could stand cold winters. Plus, at the time there were lots of positive things happening in Florida, especially in the Orlando area. My father-in-law had property to be developed near what's now the University of Central Florida, and at that time was Florida Technical University.

By the end of May, 1973 we had finished moving our whole business down there. Pasquale, Antonio and another one of my brothers-in-law, Jerry Iadipaolo, came down with all of the equipment and started doing concrete and cement work and building homes.

Jerry was born in Casalvieri, Italy, a town that borders Vicalvi. He came here in his mid-teens, and had just mastered English when the United States went to war in Europe. He was soon drafted and proudly served in the US Army. His only request was that he not be sent to fight in Italy.

He fought in the campaign in France against the Nazi occupation, and before he went back to the US, he went on leave from Germany to visit his hometown as a proud United States Army soldier. There he was welcome not only as a native son, but as an American liberator.

Jerry's stay in Florida wound up being pretty short. Anna and their six kids were still back in Detroit and he missed them too much. He just couldn't stay away. Without even telling us, one evening he got into his car and the next we heard from him is when he called us and said, "I'm back in Detroit."

That fall, my father retired at the age of 65. I remember when he called to tell me that he was going back to Italy. He said that he appreciated everything that America had done in helping him to provide for his family, and achieve for himself and all his children - for that truly was his dream - but still, he wanted to go back.

I said, "Why are you going back to Italy? You sacrificed your entire adult life. You left Italy as a businessman, you worked for twenty-five years as a construction laborer to make life better for your kids. You achieved your goals, your home is paid for. You've done well, you should enjoy the rest of your years."

His answer was that he wasn't the type to sit on the couch in front of the TV and wait to die. I told him that he didn't have to do that. Both Pasquale and I were in business,

He said, "No, I'm going to go back, I'm going to remodel our house in Italy."

He explained that he still didn't speak English very well, even though he went to night school and got his citizenship papers and passed his test. He and my mother both became American citizens and were very proud that they did so even though they were in their sixties.

My parents both went to great pains even at that age to become Americans and really become citizens. At the time, to become a citizen, they gave you a test and then you had to read and write in English. You had to know how many Congressmen were in the House of Representatives, how many were in the Senate, who was the first president and more. They were basic questions, but questions that unfortunately a lot of native born Americans would probably not be able to answer.

I remember speaking with my parents about their schooling and process of becoming a citizen and I felt very proud of them, that they made such an effort to get their citizenship.

He was a very proud individual, my father, and when he discussed business or politics, while he could express himself very well in Italian, he simply couldn't do in English.

"I'm tired of taking a backseat when it comes to a simple discussion of everyday life," he told me.

That hit home. But it's important to remember that that didn't make the United States any less than what he had felt about it all those years ago in Italy. He was thankful that his family was in a good position - that was his American dream. To have his kids all owning their own homes and own businesses.

So my father went back to Italy and lived to be ninety-four years old. Right now, my mother is ninety-eight and I still call to talk to her every Sunday and I visit her in Italy once a year. Even at her advanced age she's just as bright and spry as she ever was.

Chapter 17

Once we hit Florida things seemed to be going quite well. I finally found the warmth and sunshine that I longed for after spending over sixteen winters in Canada, Detroit and Washington, DC - no more harsh winters for me!

But while the climate may have been nice and sunny in Florida, the national climate was turning chilly. Vietnam was still a daily occurrence in the news, Nixon was dealing with Watergate and then the oil embargo began.

The entire country suffered from the embargo, but the construction industry was hit particularly hard. As the expenses grew, it became harder and harder to fuel the construction vehicles and machinery, and therefore it became increasingly tougher to make the bottom line.

In January of 1974, during all these economic woes, my first child, Luigi, was born. The American dream was a little harder to follow in those years and with the economy suffering I knew that I had little choice but to leave construction.

The Carter years were very hard for everyone. The economy was terrible and the hostage crisis really drove a knife into American pride. We were hurting not only financially, but spiritually as well.

Though I decided to leave construction, Pasquale and Antonio had decided to stay in and try and ride it out. Once the interest rates hit 18%, however, it was the final nail in the coffin. They began looking for alternatives.

Ultimately, Antonio decided to move back to Italy, along with Concetta and their daughter. Much like my father, he never gave up hope on the United States, and became a citizen before he went back to Italy, though to this day he hasn't moved back. That may change though, as his only daughter recently married a native of Vicalvi who lives in Denver, Colorado.

Pasquale stuck it out a little while longer but eventually moved back to Michigan, settling in Farmington Hills, where he and his family still live. He stayed in construction and today he builds custom homes.

He eventually had 3 kids, and is fortunate to have his son living on one side of his house, and one of his daughters on the other, all living the American dream together. I guess this is all indicative of how close our families are, as Patti and I built a home right next door to her parents.

I decided that I liked Orlando too much to leave, so I resolved that as long as I could put food on the table, I'd stay in Florida. For a lot of years, I wasn't able to do much more than that, and while I may have given up a lot of earning potential by not going back to Detroit, I enjoy life a lot more here because as I said, I really love the warmer climate.

Since construction was non-existent, I decided to go into the restaurant business. My father-in-law and his brother had a restaurant up north which they had recently sold. They convinced me that it would be good to start a new restaurant down in Florida.

This was right before my daughter Clarissa was born. Those were tough years to start a family in, and I soon discovered that the restaurant business is very demanding, and takes up a lot of your time.

Starting a restaurant also humbled me a bit. I know that it sounds mean, but at the time, I had always thought that restaurant workers were restaurant workers because they didn't want to work very hard. I didn't think that it was a very macho job, certainly not like building houses in construction. I had no idea how wrong I was.

Making the transition from the construction business to the restaurant business, took a lot of time - a lot of time with no work. I used my downtime as an opportunity to take additional courses in business administration at Florida Technological University so that I would improve my ability to run future businesses.

Two of the guys that I'd worked with in the construction business in Detroit now owned successful restaurants. My father-in-law asked them to come down to teach me the Italian restaurant business. They agreed, but their time was short.

To say that they gave me a crash course would be an understatement - they were only able to stay for less than a week to train me! We started on a Thursday, and by the following Monday they told me that I knew all that they could teach me, and they went back to Detroit. They left one of their workers with me and by the end of the week he too left.

On June 19, 1975, we opened the very first Pizza Boy Italian Restaurant in Casselberry, FL (later known as Casa Mia, which means "my house"). I was able to manage the business, and being Italian I knew what good food tasted like, so I was confident that I'd do well. It was mostly a pizzeria but we had some other dishes like veal and pasta and lasagna and sub sandwiches as well. A lot of family effort, along with help from my in-laws, allowed our restaurants to eventually become successful.

But the road to success is not always smooth. I kept my builder's license and after a couple of years, I decided that even though my restaurant was doing well, I wanted to get back into construction.

Soon after I made my decision, I was approached by a very charming, smooth talking salesman, who was moving down from Tennessee. He had a lot of experience in the home modernization business. Because of the high cost of buying a new home, people were choosing to remodel the home that they already owned instead. It seemed like home renovation was a good business to go into.

So I borrowed some money from my father and launched a home modernization business with my new partner. Shortly thereafter I had plenty of work and put ads in the newspaper with our picture, which unknowingly turned out to be a bad move.

I soon started to suspect a lack of ethics and morals in my partner, Charles Arthur Tarentino. He was half Italian and half Jewish, but I began to notice that he was Italian to Italians and Jewish to Jews. It may not sound like much, but the fact that he played both sides was the first indication of his dishonesty.

At one point he disappeared for three days because he said that money was tight. When he reappeared he was driving a brand new Cadillac. When I asked him how he could afford the car if he supposedly had financial problems, he made up an unconvincing story about how he got it.

After it became obvious that he wasn't an honest businessman, I went to my attorney so that I could withdraw from the company, giving up my equity in the process. I didn't care though - I just wanted to get out.

Things were okay for about six months, but the jobs that my former partner were supposed to complete were never finished. After I left he just never continued the work. The guy skipped town and about a year later I was approached by a plain clothes policeman in my own restaurant.

I was horrified. The policeman said that I was being charged with grand theft related to construction. I thought it was a joke. Laughing, I even said, "What I'd do, steal a wheel barrow?"

He looked at me and said, "I'm serious."

He informed me that I was being sued by all of the people whom my former partner had ripped off. Even though I was out of the company, my name was used to pull the permits on the jobs, so I was still libel for them. It was the darkest day of my life. I was booked and released in a matter of hours, but it felt like my whole life was over.

At least the policeman was a true gentleman, and understood my predicament. He let me make arrangements for my manager to stay and work my shift at Pizza Boy. I asked him if I could move my car from the front of the restaurant to the side and he let me do that as well. I then got in his car - he didn't even cuff me - and proceeded to the Seminole county jail in Sanford.

I had already called my lawyer before I left the restaurant so I made my appearance in front of the judge within hours and was on my way home around four o'clock that afternoon.

I thought I had escaped a very embarrassing situation, and that this would soon be over. However, even before I had reached my home, I heard my name announced on the radio along with the story of my arrest, and at night on the news the person who initiated the suits blew up my picture from my newspaper ads, and put it on TV.

The shame was unbearable. Never in my life had I been in a situation like this. I had to defend myself and so I hired an attorney who found out that the FBI was after my former partner in at least ten states.

Luckily, once the prosecutor who was handling the suit had found out the situation, he saw that I hadn't done anything wrong. I fully cooperated with the investigation, and ultimately was put on probation for a year, and then all of my criminal records were expunged. The incident, however, has never been expunged from my mind.

I think that it's important to mention that throughout those trials, I never once though ill of America and in fact the system of justice worked for me in the end. I continued on with my restaurants and became very successful. I was able to provide for my family and after the ordeal that I went through things became a lot more pleasant.

My good experiences in America have always outweighed the bad. I've had many business partners over the years, three of whom turned out to be very dishonest, but my faith in humanity remains as strong as ever.

A famous Roman once said, "There is goodness in everyone, in some you have to look a little harder."

Moving from one country to another, and then moving all over the United States while in the military, I was favored to look at people as friends and only look at them as an enemy if they proved to be one. There may be some bad individuals, but not all individuals are bad. It's a lot easier to go through life looking at people as friends, not enemies.

Once my pizza business began to boom, I started to open more and more restaurants, eventually developing a chain of fifteen Pizza Boys. In the afternoons, in between the lunch and dinner crowds, I would write letters to my father in Italy.

When I was finally able to write to him and tell him what a success my restaurants had become, I wound up in tears. I wanted him to see so badly that all his hard work and all his suffering had put me in a position where I owned a business.

On those tear stained pages, I wrote, "I wish you were here to see me now because you always gave me advice and probably thought that I was never really listening but I was and your advice always worked."

After I sent it, I called him to talk. He worked so hard to get us here and though during the last years of his life we were separated by distance, we weren't by love or feeling.

By now it was the mid-80s and a lot of people were moving into Florida. It seemed like my restaurants would continue to grow even more to meet the demands of an increased population, but that proved not to be the case. It was easy to open a small franchise carry-out place, so chain pizza restaurants began expanding in the area. It wasn't a good sign.

I always used fresh ingredients to make my pizzas, but the chains used soy bean fillers for the mozzarella cheese, and other cheaper, but less quality items. Then they began playing the two for one price game. They'd offer you two pizzas, but what they'd really do is downsize the size of both pies.

The area of a sixteen inch pizza is within one inch of the same area of two fourteen inch pizzas. So they were still giving you the same square inch area, but it appeared like you were getting twice as much. I could've played those games too, but I decided that that wasn't the way I wanted to go. I didn't like their games, but I also didn't have millions of dollars to buy ad time to educate the public on what was really going on.

My success in the restaurant business came at a sacrifice, which was not having a lot of time with my wife and kids. As it became apparent that I needed to start spending more time with them, and because my restaurants were losing their profitability, I decided to start selling them off.

Doing so wound up being a life changing event for me. It was in selling my restaurants that I realized that I'd really rather sell businesses than run them. After I sold the six restaurants that I had a direct interest in I then resigned from the corporate main office. I decided to start selling businesses as a career.

Chapter 18

In 1985 I got my real estate license and set up the last three restaurants that I still owned as my first three listings. Eighteen months later I had sold all three of them, and after the last was gone, I started my own company and became a business broker full time.

Obviously, it takes some time to get established in any new business, and I now had kids growing up and family needs and I wanted to maintain a certain lifestyle so for a long time I worked two jobs.

My father-in-law, Luigi, was a very outgoing person, and through his travels got to know the owner of Christini's Italian Restaurant, which is a very high class Orlando restaurant and recommended me to Chris Christini. I met with Christini and he wanted me to work at his restaurant. He had waiters from all over South America and Europe, but even though it was an Italian restaurant, he didn't have any Italians. Even Christini, whose name may sound Italian, was really Greek.

His current maître'd was American, so he wanted me for that position instead because I was 100% Italian. I started as an assistant and within a few weeks became the maître'd full time. I worked from 4 pm to 1 am, and then got some sleep and at 9:30 the next morning I was at the brokerage office learning the ropes there and honing my skills in sales.

Because I'm such an introvert I really had to work hard to get acclimated to selling businesses. My general contracting background really helped me a lot in the general knowledge department, but I also had to learn the financial part of the business.

Working both jobs was exhausting, but luckily I liked doing them both. Sometimes at the restaurant I was able to be a front waiter for large parties and got to talk a bit about the different wines that we offered. I didn't have any special schooling for the wines, but because I had grown up with wine as part of my culture, I was able to hold my own. I even knew the process of wine making which many people found interesting.

I also got to meet a lot of celebrities - Larry Bird, Billy Joel and many others ate at Christini's, and because Universal had opened their theme park, a lot of cast reunions were held there, including the casts of Leave it to Beaver and Flipper. Norman Rice, who used to run Universal Theme Parks, was also a frequent visitor.

Christini's also paid well, but the hours were harsh. It was good experience for me in other areas as well. I think working as a maître'd and having to constantly meet and speak with people from all walks of life - including some very high powered people - got me out of my shell and helped me grow into more of a talkative person, which helped me express myself in brokerage.

Within a year I slowed down and my business brokerage started to take off. Once I could support my family solely with business brokerage I left the restaurant. Business brokerage quickly became my new passion. I love it almost to an extreme. It gives me a lot of pleasure to know that everyday I'm helping people to realize their American dream.

I love to say that I create winners - I create a winner when the seller sells their business for a fair amount, and I create a winner when the buyer buys a good business to provide for their family.

Not only do I help individuals and their families, but small business really helps to grow this country and fuel its entrepreneurial spirit. It may be called small business, but when you add up all the small businesses together, they account for 95% of all the businesses in America!

I feel that I give back to my country by helping its business community. I've been blessed with so many things that I feel it's only right that I take the time to do seminars and educate people on how to buy their own business or teach people how to start their own business. You can give back in so many ways without necessarily writing a check.

I mean it's always nice when you can give money to a cause, but when you are not in that position - which many people aren't - you can also give your time to your community, and that's equally as good. Everyone has something to offer. We all do. Everyone has an experience to give, and life gives you a lot of experience.

If you have the means to do so, by all means donate financially - but that doesn't always give back as much. Sometimes it isn't financial giving that's most important. Inspiration may be a good way for those who can inspire others to do well. That's true giving, that's true elevation of the human condition.

There are so many ways to give back. Giving money may help some folks, which is commendable, but what about someone who doesn't have much money to give? Well, you could be just as giving and just as helpful and give back to your community and to your country by helping others - that's just as commendable.

You can give someone a $50 gift certificate so that they can go have a meal and I'm sure that they'll enjoy it, because

$50 should get them a pretty good meal, but once that meal is eaten, the next day the hunger comes back.

Instead you can use that same $50 to help that same person get vocational training and find ways to improve their lives. Then they won't just have $50 for a day, but will earn enough for them to eat well everyday. So it's not so much to only to give a check and say, "Here you go, go ahead and use it." It's best to train and teach people because then you give them the opportunity to be productive.

Every time I help someone buy the right business, I do it honestly and genuinely. I'm not doing anything special, I'm really just doing my job, but yet I'm helping other people in a positive way. Those people will be able to provide for their family, have a good business, provide work for others and the circle keeps going.

Can you imagine an executive who has achieved a high status, with a lot of experience, donating their time at the National Entrepreneur Center, or doing seminars and other things so often that they spend years and years not doing any work, but are instead sharing their wealth of knowledge in their field?

They're not writing a check, instead, they are being useful citizens. They are giving back even after they've retired, after their earnings are done, because they don't need them anymore. They've retired, but they are fruitful, they are useful. But you don't have to be an executive to do such a thing, all of us can do it. That's how to truly give back in the most natural and simple way.

That's wonderful if you can give a lot of money. We should all give as much as we can, but that's not the only way to give back. It doesn't have to be monetary; it can be your skills, your intellect and your knowledge. Those too will be appreciated.

Chapter 19

I quickly grew to love business brokerage once I saw what I could achieve with it as my career. One day in 1993 I got a call from a southerner with a very heavy South Carolinian parlance. He wanted to know if I had an interest in talking to him about buying into the Sunbelt Business Broker franchise.

At that time I had just finished negotiations with VR Business Brokers. They were the main national brokerage firm at the time, but I decided not to go with them. When I looked into them I saw that they were declining in their number of franchisees, eventually going from over two hundred offices down to around seventy. I saw that their fee structure made it impossible to sustain a business. Even though I didn't join them, I was still interested in growing my business by joining a larger franchise, so when I received the call I agreed to the meeting and I was ready that same afternoon.

Sunbelt's founder, Ed Pendarvis, and his partner, Dennis D'Annunzio, had been in Tampa talking with other business brokers about their franchise but were unsuccessful. They were about to leave Florida empty handed, but Ed didn't want to give up without having sold a single franchise, so he called me.

At the time, Sunbelt only had eighteen offices, but I had always felt that if one of something is good, then one plus one is better. It was that multiple thinking that allowed me to grow my restaurants - building one at a time was profitable, but building several was more profitable. It's the same with business brokerage offices.

I thought that what they were offering looked good, so I bought into Sunbelt and it was a good decision, one of the best I'd ever made. I kept my business growing until I had enough money to buy more franchise areas and by the time that I was done I was running ten and a half counties in central Florida as my Sunbelt franchise area.

I empower everyone who works with me at Sunbelt to stay independent. In fact, the people that work with me are not really my employees. They are fellow workers, they are independent contractors. When licensed in Florida, a real estate agent's license must be placed under a licensed broker, otherwise they'd be on payroll.

So really, the people who work with me all have their own businesses, but work under Sunbelt. I have a company that helps people be in business. So all of the licensed agents that work in my company are independent contractors and in essence they are each their own boss.

I always say to people that if a boy who started at eight years old hauling manure out to the field can come to America and now own his own business and help others to own their own businesses, then it should be easy for someone who starts out in this country with a lot more then I started out with to accomplish incredible things. The opportunity is out there for everyone, and with the proper training and the proper work ethic, anyone can succeed.

I always tell my clients, and the people who attend my seminars, "Look, if I can do it, I know you can."

Although in high school I worked as a sales clerk, I always valued other types of work - construction, building etc. But sales were never my strong suit. I never believed I could sell anything unless I believed that the product was needed and valuable. Even when I had my restaurants, I valued the kitchen much more than the front, even though both are equally important.

Being an introvert, I could never envision myself selling anything. Then again, I also never envisioned hosting a radio talk show either, but today I not only do both, but I run a real estate company too.

When necessity calls for you to do something different, you need to muster up the courage to do it. In order to realize your dream you'll encounter things that are difficult, but you must get through them. The reward will be much greater than the trial.

I truly believe that being more of an introvert by nature has been my strong suit in helping people to find the right business to buy. I'm not there to talk someone into buying what I think is right, but rather I'm there to listen to them and find out what they want. I think of myself as more of a facilitator than a salesman. I value myself more in that role.

I don't think of myself as selling anything. I consider what I do to be helping other people. Some want to buy a business, but don't know what the right business is for them, and some want to sell their business because they're retiring or whatever the reason, and need to get a good value on their lifetime of equity.

What I do is get all the information about a business that I can. I educate myself about the business so that I can represent it properly and present it to a potential buyer. I help work out the mechanics - how to do it, how to pay for it, and figure out how to put it all together and make it happen.

I help someone sell their business for good money, for a fair price and go on with their goals and I help someone to buy a good business that will provide for them and their family and provide jobs for others. Either way, I help people get to their goal line, and when I get those people to the goal line, I get to the goal line myself.

I help a lot of immigrants - *legal* immigrants - who are coming into this country and need to buy their first business in America. I try to give advice to them when they're buying a business, and one of the most important things I tell them is that if you're buying a business, one of the things is that you should know is the language that you going to be doing business in.

There are a good number of examples of those who don't assimilate with the culture or learn the language who are not as successful as those that do. That is a proven fact. I don't have to go anywhere outside of my own Italian heritage. It was much harder for those who came to this country later in life to learn the language and to speak properly, and they had a harder time acclimating and getting their own businesses and accumulating wealth and living comfortably than those that came here at a younger age.

As a child, in five or six months you can do a pretty good job of learning English. You'll be out there able to communicate with the other children at a very fast pace. As you get older, into your teens and later, it might take you a few months longer but still within a year's time you will do a very good job learning English.

Younger immigrants assimilate easier because when you come here at a younger age it's easier to learn the language. It's easier to speak clearly and get an education in this country and once you start assimilating it's much easier to be successful in business and in every aspect of life.

As you get into your twenties, thirties, forties, well it could take a year or two years or more. You'll probably need extra schooling at night, because you also need to keep a job during the day.

It's hard, and it may be a lot easier just to keep your native language, but learning English is the way that all of the previous immigrants who came into this country did it, and they were all proud to learn English and become a part of this nation.

I also advise people looking to immigrate that if they want to become citizens, then they should know the laws. My parents became citizens of the United States in their sixties. They went to school so that they could learn English and understand the Constitution and what it meant. They may have spoken in broken English but they went to school to try to assimilate and become good citizens of this country.

They didn't say, "You should teach me in Italian because I don't know how to speak English, and don't want to learn."

I can't stress enough how important it is to assimilate into the American culture, to understand the laws, to respect those laws and to benefit by those laws. So to those who want to say, "I want to be taught in my native language." Too bad. This is an English-speaking country.

How much money do we already spend to teach a language other than English in our schools, when the goal is to have the students speak English? Why do we hire extra teachers to only communicate in a foreign language when that only delays the process of learning English?

We're at the point where if we have twenty Spanish speaking students, and twenty English speaking students, we have to furnish a bilingual teacher, because it's politically correct. But do we double the time so that both of the languages can be taught in an equal amount of time? No - instead we split the learning time in half, so no one is benefiting in the process, and our children - both English and Spanish speaking - have only half the time to get an education.

It's okay to accommodate in some fashion, but to start teaching in another language entirely - all that does is disrupt the whole system for all of the people who came over to this country. I went to school learning English with not only Italian kids, but French, Polish, German and many other nationalities. We weren't taught in Italian, French, German, Polish or anything else, we were taught in English! That's what makes a country great, everybody learns the same language, everybody speaks the same language and everyone benefits.

Once you come into this country, assimilation is really a must and if you don't think that it's important, then you're not going to be successful and you're certainly not a good citizen. If the people who come here truly love this country, then they'll want to assimilate into the culture. In my estimation, if you don't want to assimilate into this country then you really have no business being here.

It might sound a little harsh, but if you don't want to come to this country to be a part of it, then you should leave. If you can't find it in yourself to put out the effort to become a citizen, then why should we even let you into this country?

If we don't promote assimilation, are we not promoting segregation? The goal of every legal immigrant who comes to this country is to be an American. It's the goal of the illegal alien to take all of the benefits of America, but not become an American, and that we shouldn't stand for.

Is it possible to assimilate and still keep your cultural identity? Of course it is! I haven't lost my Italian identity - but I'm an American, I live here, and I love this country. When I go back to Italy, I speak Italian, but when I'm in America, I speak in English!

Sure, sometimes when I'm speaking with a fellow Italian we may switch to our native tongue. Sometimes it's because of nostalgia, and sometimes it's just easier to communicate in Italian, but in everyday life I speak English. I certainly don't go around demanding that every sign, billboard and piece of text should be in Italian as well.

If things are becoming bilingual - English and Spanish, then why not Italian? What about German? French? Chinese? Swahili? Where do we stop? Do we need to make sure that every language ever spoken is represented?

This is America, - be an American! You've heard the expression, "When in Rome do as the Romans do." Well if you're in America, do as the Americans do. That's the way it should be! A country simply can't keep its unity if its citizens can't all speak a common language, it's like the Tower of Babel - you can't build anything great if no one can communicate with each other.

If we start having different languages and different documentations in this country then that's strength's going to deteriorate. All citizens of a country - no matter what the nation - need to be able to speak the same common language, otherwise things can't get done.

People should remember what this country is and what it's done. You should not only remember everything about your country, but you should also appreciate why you are here. What duties do you have as a citizen of this country? If you don't understand that, then how can you be a good citizen? If you don't assimilate, you really can't be one.

When I sell businesses to immigrants I tell them that it's nearly impossible to be successful if you don't know how to communicate. Even if you have a simple business where you stand behind a counter, and your customer brings the merchandise to you, someone could still stop by and ask you for directions.

What if you don't know how to communicate? You can't help someone who asks if you have a different brand. Quite simply, if you can't communicate with your customers, how successful do you really think you're going to be with your business?

There are times when I have to sell businesses for people who made the wrong decision to buy because they didn't take the time to learn to communicate. Unfortunately they're going to have to take a loss in most cases because if they're not communicating, they're not doing right by their business, so the profitability goes down and therefore their business is worth less.

Chapter 20

Every time Ed Pendarvis - who is now my good friend - comes to do training here in Florida, he always says, "I love being back in paradise." I agree with him one hundred percent.

I've been blessed to move to Orlando, Florida. What more could one ask for then to come to the United States and then end up living in tropical paradise, surrounded by all of the great things that America has to offer and to have achieved success in business?

What one perceives as success - it could be having a home, having a family, having a nice car - is relative, I think, to each and every one of us. For some of us its a million dollars in the bank, but for others like myself, being a good person is one's success. Being looked at as a good human being in your community is what I consider to be success.

For some of us, success is very simple. I have my family, I'm well-off, and I'm very happy. My success is that I have my own business; I've achieved being my own boss. For me, it was when I set foot in this country. That in itself was where I wanted to go, where I wanted to be. It's where my parents and my whole family wanted to be.

Going into business, being able to employ people, to be able to provide for my family, is success - being able to be my own boss. How did I achieve my success? It's no big mystery. I worked, I applied myself, I've always tried to do what is right, and of course I think I was helped by the fact that I strongly believe that honesty is really the best policy.

In fact it was a Roman, a couple thousand years ago, who said, "No man becomes successful by stepping on others. Success is not achieved by trampling over others to get to the top. Success is achieved by helping others. That will in turn help you."

I'm really thankful that I've found a way to earn a living by truly helping others. To me, that's fantastic! I enjoy what I do - it's the kind of job that I think I will do well into my years, as long as I have the mental clarity and the health to move around. If I have the same longevity as my parents, living into my nineties, I look forward to working well past retirement I don't see my career ending at 65. Hopefully I'll be able to keep helping people buy the right business to provide for their families.

I absolutely believe that the American dream is here for anyone who wants it. There isn't anyone in this country who can say that the dream is only for others. The Founding Fathers first fought to gain freedom for themselves, and then less than a hundred years later the Union fought against itself to ensure that the dream of its freedoms would be realized by all its citizens. If an outsider like myself can come and achieve the dream, then anyone can.

The only ones who say that the dream isn't for them, or that the opportunities aren't there, are the ones who don't really have the drive or desire to work hard and succeed. They'd rather just take the easier choice and waste their time complaining rather than taking the steps to better themselves.

Does everyone have the aspiration or the willingness? No - but it's still there. This country is the only country that says that minorities can receive help to rise above their minority status - be it race, gender, etc.

No other country in the world says to anyone, "At some point you weren't on an equal basis, so we're going to give you the opportunity to rise up to the level that you deserve." For no other reason, that makes this country better than any other in the world.

But on the other side of that coin, taking and redistributing the wealth and giving it to those who don't want to work for it, takes away the incentive of those who work hard to achieve it. By doing so we degrade the lives of those who take the charity and that takes away the drive - why would you want to work hard if the government will still reward you?

I've heard some cynics say, "We shouldn't have poverty in this country, we should give. We should give to the homeless, we should build shelters."

That is a noble statement, it is a noble cause. It sounds great, but why not teach these people how to be productive? I think that some in politics want dependence on government because if they have a dependant constituency, they can gain votes. They want their people to say, "The government gives me a paycheck, and they give me these programs and they really help me out."

They don't realize that by doing this they are creating dependency. A dependent state is a terrible thing for a human being to be in. To make the people dependent upon the government for the rest of their lives, instead of teaching them to be productive is demeaning. It's tragic but that's what some politics foster. They foster dependency, not independency. If the government wants to establish a welfare state, what they're really doing is demeaning the value of life to their citizens.

To give someone a free meal because they're in need - that's a good thing. It's being generous. It's giving. But to create dependency is an evil thing, and governments that create dependency, are almost creating slaves in a way. If people become too dependent on government, that's bad.

As Thomas Jefferson said, "Any government strong enough to give you everything you want is strong enough to take everything you have."

I find it almost demeaning to put someone in a position of dependency. It serves no purpose to create a dependant society - it only serves the politicians to get votes - "look what we do for you" But that only creates nonproductive voters, not good citizens.

I would rather see a politician with a philosophy that says, "Let me help the constituents become productive. Let me help them to not only be productive for themselves, but to even create jobs for others."

The government should be there to help and support the people, but not make them dependent. I hold these beliefs, because I feel that there is an inherent pride in every human being and to receive welfare is to create a dependency that makes one feel worthless.

There's a time when a handout is needed, and there's a time to teach those how to earn their meal, to work for their food, for their well-being. In order to stay great, you can never lose the incentive for people to achieve.

I think that the best way to solve the welfare problem is to teach people to create and feel worthwhile. To work hard instead of rewarding those that wanted to just sit around and collect. That is the way to do it, not have a hand in dependency.

We all strive to be independent. We want to be fruitful, we want to be productive. We can't give in to those that foster the belief that government is a provider. I know that I could spend my dollars in a better way and get a much better return than the ones I send to Washington. I don't feel that I get my services for the dollars worth that I spend.

If the government spent or earmarked funds so that those in need can learn to be productive and earn a living, it will give them self respect and high goals and a better outlook on life. Our welfare program gives a man a fish; I think it should teach him how to fish.

It's the opportunity that this country offers that makes it so wonderful. I believe that our current welfare system can be harmful because of the dependence that it creates, and yet I also believe that it's noble to help those less fortunate. So how to rectify the two?

Tax money should not just go to food stamps and other welfare benefits, but in order to receive those benefits, you must be enrolled in an adult education or vocational program. The state will support you, but only if you prove that you are attempting to better yourself and are putting out an effort to learn something. I'm not saying that we should deprive poor people of food or shelter, but there needs to be an effort on their part to better themselves.

It might even cost more at first to fund school systems for welfare recipients, but as people begin to graduate from vocational schools, they will no longer be dependent on the government, so over time less money will be spent. We'll begin to have more productive citizens who participate in the tax system, thereby creating more revenue and contributing to the American economy.

We should keep educating people, all people, to be productive and be independent. That's what makes this country great. It is the ingenuity. We've all heard about American ingenuity. We've all heard about American independence - the dream of owning your own business and being your own boss. We all have the opportunity to be our own boss. We all have the opportunity to create jobs for others. And so we should take it.

Vicalvi during the war - Notice the Red Cross painted on the castle

Monte Cassino destroyed and rebuilt

My Father's Drivers License

Enrico Ferrari at 40

Anna Maria Saurini Ferrari

1952 - Left to Right Anna Igida and Ortensia
Pasquale and Anna Maria

Left to Right Franco, Loreta and Concetta

1956 Left to Right Franco with Sisters Concetta and Loreta

My First Holy Communion in Italy Age 8

May 1954 - Our Month of the Rosary
Special Alter prepared at home

Friends visiting our house before we left Italy

The Vulcania - The ship that brought me to America

1958 - Playing the Accordion at Age 12

1961 - Left to Right: My brother Pasquale, My father Enrico, and I

1963 - Left to Right: Franco, Ivana, Anthony, Kathy, and Ortensia

1967 – Military Service

Patti and I visting Italy

Franco and Patti Ferrari, Clarissa and Robert Borrelli,
and Margaret and Luigi Ferrari in Orlando FL

Me with my 98 year old mother Anna Maria in Italy

PART II

What Made This Country Great, and What Will Tear It Apart

Chapter 21

As a business broker I have the pleasure to sell a lot of businesses to foreign nationals so that they can obtain a visa to come to this country legally. I've been there myself - twice in fact - waiting endlessly to go through the legal process, and so I do my part to help others to come to this great country so that they can benefit and achieve like I have.

I do my part to help legal immigrants enter this country, and so I must say that the idea that we should let illegal aliens in, while those who love and honor this country enough to want to come in the right, legal way, is unconscionable.

I have seen good, decent immigrants get so frustrated when they see illegal aliens get more rights then they have that I've heard them say "Maybe I should give up and take the illegal route," and it breaks my heart.

It needs to be told that this country welcomes people. Immigrants like myself are blessed that we have earned - that's right - earned - the privilege to come to this country and enjoy the fruits of the United States of America. Those who want to gain entry into this country need to do it legally. To do so otherwise is to invite disaster.

Right now we have an illegal immigration problem - the key word here being "illegal." There's a lot of deception when it comes to arguments for illegal immigration - the most blatant of which is that they like to drop the word "illegal" and only say "immigrant." They say that everyone in America is descended from an immigrant - and they're right - but they forget that those were *legal* immigrants.

Yes, it's true that this country was built by immigrants, but once again it was built by legal immigrants - law abiding immigrants. Sure, some went astray and some didn't obey the laws and we have many incidents where people have been incarcerated, but the point is that at least those who had to go through the process of waiting their turn to gain entry had to be scrutinized, and had to be legitimate, good citizens with no record of illegal infractions. Only then could they gain entry into this country.

We have immigration laws, we have an immigration system. We've had it for over a hundred years. I came through those immigration laws. And so did a lot of people. So did all the Europeans who came here and the Chinese later on and all the other nationalities.

If you follow the immigration system, then everything is orderly, everything is right, and the country fosters and prospers and it keeps going. Immigration laws have worked for this country, but now all of a sudden we have to disregard them because millions are breaking them? That's not the way it should be.

Why do the politicians say that it is all right to let illegals stay? Why do they think that we should reward them for their tenacity in getting into the United States? There's a process for a reason. There's a way to come to this country legally - through application, through screening, through all of the ways that are already in place to come here legally.

For illegal aliens to cross our borders and then expect us to cater to them is absurd. When I came to this country, as many other immigrants did, I went through the legal process and then assimilated into the culture of the country. In fact, all immigrants should strive to do all that they can to assimilate into the culture and be productive American citizens. Meanwhile illegals just take and take without ever giving back.

Why would you disrespect the laws if you wanted to be here and be a productive citizen? Why would you come here and only want to take from this country and not give back your fair share? What message are we sending to all of the people who have been waiting for years to legally become citizens of this country? They'd be better off sneaking in? Is that really the message that we want to get across?

I can't condone coming into this country illegally. It isn't right. It abuses the good system that we have. I don't think that it's right for people to want to come here and abuse the system by not contributing, not paying their fair share of taxes. I don't even think its right for churches or cities to give sanctuary. When you do that, basically you're saying that it's okay to break the law. If someone else wants to break the law, you can go ahead.

Illegal aliens break the law with the first step they take into the country, and it just leads to more illegal acts, which we are seeing more and more of. The whole thing leads to a breakdown of society if you disrespect the law.

One of the things that I always admired about the United States was that its people have respect for the law. In Italy my experience was that if somebody had to stand in line for something, like at the bank, it was just a mob. Whoever got the attention of the teller first got served. There was no respect for the law. Thank God that has changed.

I remember that as a child - and maybe it was because the poor people, having suffered through the war, felt they had to push and be forceful to get service - but coming to the

United States and seeing the orderly way people did things was a delightful change.

To simply be respected as a human being - you get in line and stand behind the person in front of you and not try to get in front of them. Law and order make this country great. We're a nation of laws. Of course where you have laws, you have lawbreakers, but at least if you have a lawbreaker that's a citizen, you have recourse against that citizen. That's the way it's supposed to be done. You don't have citizens who come in, take advantage and then run away!

I don't think that you embark on any journey by breaking the law. If you do, you've already started on shaky ground. And you know what happens to anything that is not built on a solid foundation? It's not going to stand up to the test of time.

I can't see anyone sneaking in and taking what they want and still maintaining a sense of morality. You may do something unethical or immoral and feel okay with it on the surface, but in your heart you know, in your mind, you know, and so it's going to eat away at you in some fashion. It will never be right even if you get away with it, or think that you've gotten away with it.

Those who sneak in aren't really breaking the law to become Americans - they don't want to become Americans. What they want is for Americans to give them what they think they're owed in some bizarre way. They think that because America is a rich and abundant country it's only right that they should give all of their wealth to those less fortunate (of course we do, and then we get complaints that we shouldn't interfere with other countries.)

What illegal aliens don't understand - or don't want to understand - is that America isn't a rich country simply by the grace of God. Americans work hard for all that they achieve. They like to paint a picture that Americans are selfish for wanting to keep what they earn and not give it to those who don't earn it.

Illegal aliens have no pride in this country, no patriotism, they don't want to be proud Americans like the legal immigrants who have to go through the right channels and wait years for the privilege of becoming Americans. They resent America for what it has and only want to siphon off what they can.

They want to take what they can and say, "I still want to be what I am. I don't want your rules - I just want your money. I just want your place, where you live, I want to come and make money. In fact I don't even want to stay here; I'll take your money and send it back home." That's not right.

Sure it's easier to do things that way, but it's not the right way. With that mentality, why get a job and work hard when you can go rob a bank? Why even bother to leave your own country if you want to take things illegally?

Why not give everyone free access to come into this country - open up the borders! Well in doing so you wouldn't know who you're letting in, which in this time of terrorism is simply the worst thing you could possibly do. You need to know who is in your country; you need to know who's in your house.

I think it's just unconscionable for people to not want to protect the borders of this country. You can't leave the borders unguarded and let anyone that wants to come in to do so. I'm sure there are those that want to come to this country and have good intentions, but there is a rule and there is a procedure and they should follow it.

If you have millions of people coming in freely across the border, then you may have some well-intentioned people that just want a better life, but you also have those who would come here just to do devastating harm. Terrorists are all over. Nowadays especially, this country has to always be on guard and if you don't protect your borders and protect your property then the terrorists can gain entry and do harm to all of us.

We're concerned about protecting Iraqis from terrorists, we're concerned about protecting Afghanis from al-Qaeda and the Taliban, we're concerned about protecting life all over the world - all of which is noble - but we're much less protective of our own country. Always remember that if illegals can find a way to sneak into this county, then terrorists can slip in the same way.

When you have unguarded borders, you don't know who is coming in. When you have politicians who only worry about their next vote instead of what's right for the country, society falters. When you have people that are unaccountable or don't feel they should be accountable for their actions you have a further deterioration of society.

One only has to look at Europe to see how an open border policy can be disruptive. Europe has gone downhill since they opened up their borders. Now the countries of the EU are losing control over who enters and leaves, and they're realizing that because of the free borders of the European Union, there's a lot of dissension and a lot of people going from one country to another. They don't assimilate and because of that, they're having some major problems.

Whenever I travel abroad I witness non-natives disobeying local laws, pan handling and simply committing crimes before escaping back into their home country. There are places in Italy today where you can't go shopping without being accosted by beggars who will literally grab you and pull you aside and you can barely walk the sidewalks because they're being taken up by illegal merchants selling their wares on blankets. They just plop down and take over.

Criminals in the Eastern Bloc countries - namely Albania and Romania - have been crossing over into Italy, Germany, Holland and Belgium, raising their crime rates, and committing horrible acts such as kidnapping - taking their helpless victims back over the border.

France is having a major problem with Muslim illegal aliens who come over from North Africa, and from there they're free to travel through all of Europe. Whenever you hear someone in America talk about opening the borders, just remember those bombings in England and Spain!

What is right for one citizen is right for the next. What is wrong for one citizen is wrong for the next. We're all equal, we should be treated equal and even in coming into this country that is the rule.

The rule is the rule, the law is the law. You apply and you come into this country in an orderly fashion - we know who is here, we know who is paying taxes and we know who is breaking our laws because they're all accountable.

Chapter 22

I've heard some proponents of illegal immigration try to make an argument simply by saying, "What would Jesus do?"

I think that Jesus would want people to respect the law and He even said as much, "Render to Caesar the things that are Caesar's and to God the things that are God's."

If Caesar is the law of the land and he said render unto Caesar what is Caeser's, then I would interpret that as: The United States has borders, you should respect them. The United States has a tax system, you should respect it and pay your fair share.

Some argue that because we're such a bountiful country, we should give free food to those that don't have anything. They say that we should do all we can to help everyone who needs it because we are all citizens of the world. Excuse me? Yes, we're all citizens of the world, but this country is a country and it has its laws.

If we're all citizens of the world then why do we have countries trying to go against the United States? Why is it that we just can't go to over to any country that we want and take whatever resources we need?

If we're all citizens of the world then why aren't we allowed to just go and take gold from anywhere in the world that we want or to the Middle East and take all the oil that we want. If we're all citizens of the world then anyone from any country should be able to take whatever resources or food that they need from any country they want.

That just isn't done. So why do our politicians and pro-illegals feel that you should let in anyone who wants to come in? Let's just give them amnesty, let's just get them on the track to becoming a citizen, and forget about those who love this country enough to take the time to come in legally.

For any politician to say that we should just let illegals in or give amnesty to the ones who've already snuck in isn't being right to all of those who are working hard and have sacrificed to come here the right, legal way. That's like telling me that what I did, my father did, my family - we were stupid. We should have just come on over. What do you mean you kept the family separated? Separated for years? Sacrificed? Foolish! Just come on over!

Of course I'd love for everyone to be in good standing and to have access to all of the wonderful things that we have in this country. I love this country because of all those things, it's why I spent my whole childhood yearning to be here, but I think we're better off teaching other countries and their citizens how to gain in their own country, instead of sneaking over here and upsetting and ruining the system that we have here. If we let in everyone who could benefit from our system, the system would collapse - it's already starting to.

In 1787 Alexander Tyler, a history professor at the University of Edinburgh said about the fall of Athens, "A democracy is always temporary in nature; it simply cannot exist as a permanent for of government."

He pointed out that at some point in the lifespan of a democracy, the public will realize that if they vote for the candidate who will give them the most benefits from the

Treasury, then they can freely take from the government. This will in turn lead to a loose fiscal policy, resulting in a collapse and a dictatorship.

He tracked the phases of democracy as going from bondage to faith, faith to courage, courage to liberty, liberty to abundance, abundance to complacency, complacency to apathy, apathy to dependence and finally dependence back into bondage. Right now we're mired in apathy - we must not slip down into the final stage, we must not lose our democracy.

Chapter 23

The real tragedy with the illegal immigration problem is that the politicians are turning a blind eye to it and they're going to ruin this country by not enforcing the law. We need to enforce the laws that we already have on the books - we have laws that were written to protect our borders, but they are being ignored.

Too many of our elected representatives have acted really shamefully and have tried to confuse the issue of immigration by attempting to reward those who trespass over our borders illegally, thereby punishing the thousands who are currently going through the proper legal channels to obtain their visa to enter the United States.

When those politicians look the other way - who are they serving? Are they serving their constituents? Their law abiding citizens, those who have a legal right to be here, or are they serving the interests of those in the country who support illegals?

If you are charged with protecting this country, it doesn't matter if you're a Republican or if you're a Democrat, or if you're independent, if you're in local government, state government or the federal government. When you're an elected official, you have the responsibility to protect the citizens of this country and if you don't do that than you are not a patriot - you're not performing your job and you should be voted out.

I equate someone breaking into the United States with someone breaking into my house and I challenge those politicians who think that illegal aliens should have the right to come into this country and take advantage of all of the things that our legal immigrants, naturalized citizens and American born citizens pay taxes for to leave the doors of their homes wide open.

The legal American pays taxes, health insurance, car insurance, and is responsible to all the laws of this country. Illegal aliens, however, don't pay their fair share, do not have auto insurance, or even a license. They don't pay health insurance, instead they get free medical care. It's the legal American citizen who's at a disadvantage, not the illegal alien. On an even playing field, the illegal alien would not work for the same dollar amount that they do now - they couldn't afford it.

Illegal aliens come in and usurp those monies by not paying their fair share of taxes when they work, taking free schooling, going to the emergency room, and a myriad of other things that they take advantage of. They say it can't be done - you can't take twelve million people all at one time and send them back. No, of course not, but you shouldn't be giving them licenses and legitimizing their legal status here. Why is it that anyone who comes across the border can get a credit card, can get a driver's license in some states, and can even get sanctuary from some cities?

I'm very, very disheartened that the Bank of America has started a program to give illegal aliens credit cards, which is simply unbelievable. You shouldn't be giving them credit cards to legitimize their illegal status. Now, I'm sure that the real motivations here is money - the more people who can get a card, the more people who will owe money to the bank, which is shameful in and of itself, but even so, if I want to get a credit card and I don't have a social security card or even a social security number, I should not be able to get it. But, it's a different standard for illegal aliens.

It's another standard for illegal aliens to receive special tuition rights for their children to go to college. For illegals to sneak in and then have their kids able to go to college and pay in-state tuitions around the country makes no sense. If a Floridian wants to go to school in Michigan, they have to pay out of state tuition. How can you penalize the citizens of this country while rewarding the illegal aliens - the law breakers! That's not right.

I propose that all the politicians, and all the people who believe in open borders should leave their houses, leave their doors wide open so that anyone, any poor person who wants to come in and take whatever they want, should be able to do so. Would you allow anyone walking your house to just come in, go into your refrigerator and take whatever they need, eat whatever and drink whatever they please?

If you believe that we should not enforce the immigration laws, then I challenge you not to enforce the right to protect your own home, your own family, your own property.

Leave your house open so that anyone can come in and take whatever they want to eat, or whatever they want to drink. Maybe they like your TV better then the one they have, so now everybody should share and they can take your nice TV.

Doesn't sound very fair when you think about your personal home and hard earned possessions, does it? But everything in this country was earned by people like you working hard. Sure, it may be more abstract and therefore it may be harder to feel the same way, but all of the wonderful things that this country has - schools, hospitals, police, defense, the postal service, the highway service, national parks - and on and on and on - are all earned.

You work hard and you pay taxes and those taxes pay for all those things. You own all those things. And you should feel the same sense of pride and ownership for all of those things as you do for your home, your car, and everything else that you work hard to earn.

I don't think that you would let that happen in your house, so why should we let it happen in our country? If you think of this country as your house, then I don't think that any American citizen would allow strangers to come on in and take what they wish, yet our politicians feel that since we are all citizens of the world that anyone should have the freedom to come into the country and take whatever they want.

It's very self-serving because I'm sure that those same politicians wouldn't let an illegals come into their home on that basis, but hey, it's your tax dollars and so if they can get a vote from the illegal aliens coming in, then why should they care?

Naturally those would be illegal votes - but I don't think that it's stopped some of these politicians. Maybe they're looking for additional votes and so that is their motive.

Maybe that's the motive, and maybe not, but attempting to reward all those who've snuck in doesn't seem right. The people - the majority anyway - have already spoken and they've stated that they don't want the amnesty, they - we - want our country protected, we want the borders protected. Our politicians, however, still seem bent on wanting to reward those who break the law instead of rewarding those who abide by it.

They want to reward the illegals who break our laws. They also want to force those who respect and abide by the law, by following the immigration laws, into even longer years of hardship waiting to come here legally. Stepping on people on the climb to the top may be a common strategy for most politicians, but this time they're stepping on approximately 300 million legal Americans, to win the favor of what? Twelve million illegal trespassers? So that they could get 12 million illegal votes?

The people who either by birthright or by legal status have the right to reside in the United States are being mistreated. Every American politician needs to reread the Constitution and be reminded that they were elected to serve and represent Americans - the citizens of this country.

How can the citizens of this country continue to believe in our system and our laws while they see that this is happening? Our politicians' behavior is eroding the faith of the citizens of the United States of America. The faith of the citizens who love it and it hold dear. These are things that are going to bring down our great society if we don't guard against it and prevent it.

If we had more patriots than politicians in Washington, and in the state and city governments we wouldn't even be talking about the rights of illegal aliens. We'd have other issues to be concerned about like improving life for the legal citizens of America.

I'd like to say that the politicians were the only ones fostering illegals, but the businesses that are breaking the law by hiring illegals and forcing them to work for criminally low wages, and the unions who are only after headcounts for votes are also part of the problem.

I challenge those businesses that hire illegal aliens. I challenge them to hire real Americans. I challenge them to pay those Americans a decent wage. I challenge the unions of this country to look out for the American worker whom they were formed to protect, and not the illegal worker who threatens them.

The unions were once the darlings of America. They helped the downtrodden, they helped those who were poor, they helped the working class, they helped those who were trying to eke out a living and were not being paid a fair wage. They were great; they did a lot of important things for this country and its citizens. They did a lot of wonderful things and elevated the pay grade and the lifestyle for the society.

Today, I'm ashamed to say, the unions are almost like shakedown artists. I believe, however, that the Unions can rise up and help again. It would be nice if the Unions said that to be a Union member you must be a legal immigrant or a legal resident. The Unions should only accept and protect those in their membership who are here legally. To help and protect illegal, undocumented workers simply for votes and dues is criminal.

They need to stop having Union drives, where they don't care who they get to join up whether they're legal or illegal. As long as their members pay their dues the Unions don't care. Illegals can go back to their home country and then when they return, they'll just charge them another reentry fee.

The Unions just want more members; they don't care where they come from. The Unions are no different than the politicians who wish to let in every illegal alien who wants to just so they can get their vote. And as I've mentioned before, how can you vote legally if you are not a legal citizen? That means that there must be a lot of fraud in the voting system.

So when you hear that they're paying people to go vote over and over again - that's just crazy! It's not legal, and it shouldn't be done. The Unions are in bed with this illegal problem and they should be held accountable. The politicians who don't want to protect our borders, they too should be held accountable.

Chapter 24

It's been established that the majority of the wages paid to illegal aliens do not stay in this country, so our economy winds up suffering because the money that they take is being sent back and spent in their home countries.

Because of this, illegal immigration is fostered by other countries - namely Mexico, which establishes Mexican consulates in all major US cities and makes it easier for illegals to find ways to circumvent the system. One only has to look at the number of Mexican consulates ten years ago versus today. It takes a lot of employees to take care of fifteen million illegals, and all this goes unchecked because it's not illegal to have a consulate, but it's their services to the illegals that are against the law.

MALDEF - the Mexican American Legal Defense and Education Fund - attacks our right to free speech by calling it hate speech. Any time someone speaks out against illegal immigration they cry "racist!" They say that by discussing illegal immigration, talk radio hosts are inciting the issue. How dare they!

Isn't it hateful to break into someone else's country? To speak the truth is hate speech, but breaking the immigration laws is okay? It's hate speech for MALDEF to create hate against legal citizens from illegal aliens, but they get away with it because of political correctness.

Political correctness has to end. It promotes dishonesty and it's destroying this country. In order to be politically correct you have to shade, embellish or hide the truth. Do we value the truth or value PC? If I can't describe something truthfully because it may offend someone then it forces me to lie. What offends me is when I cannot speak the truth. How do we speak anymore if we have to use generalities? Are people so weak that they are afraid that mere words will destroy them?

Political correctness does not allow us to say illegal alien - we have to choose words now so we don't offend law breakers. Illegal aliens are now "undocumented individuals."

They don't really have a leg to stand on, so pro-illegals need to confuse the argument by pulling at emotional strings like the "everyone is an immigrant" strategy, or acting as if illegal aliens are the only immigrants entering this country. They paint the picture that Americans are selfish, lazy snobs with no compassion for other people. Of course if you've gotten this far into the book, you know what an enormous falsehood that is.

They like to pretend that historically the United States let plenty of immigrants in, and only recently have decided to close the borders and block immigrants from entering. It's ludicrous. In fact, every year for the last twenty years, the United States has let in more legal immigrants then the rest of the world combined!

And of course the same people who want to sneak in, or defend those who want to sneak in are the same people who love to bash America. Well, if America is so bad, then why come here? Maybe it comes from a guilty conscience - they'd feel bad stealing from a good country, so they need to pretend that America is bad, so it's a little easier to take from her.

I don't see a line of Americans leaving this country because it's a bad place to live. I don't see a line of people breaking the laws to get into Russia or to get into Iraq or Iran or North Korea or China. I don't see people breaking the laws of immigration to get into those countries. I only see lines of people illegally coming into this country

I equate coming here illegally with raping the country. Now that may sound strong, but think about it for a moment - If you say that you love this country but sneak in here illegally then you don't really love this country, you just want to take advantage of her.

If you see America as a beautiful woman then you love her. You don't violate her by taking her just because you want to. But that's what the illegals are doing to this country when they violate the laws by coming in illegally.

Maybe I am too strict, but I'll say one thing - if you are not a law-abiding citizen, if you simply come here and take what you want without any respect for the law, then you can never be a citizen. What you're doing is usurping the American system. You're not one who wants to assimilate and do things for the good of the country

Ultimately, the message that I want to get across is that this is the best country in the world. However, if we want to keep it the best country in the world then we need to protect it. It's important to get this message across because I really do love the United States. I love this country. I love what it stands for. It stands for freedom, it stands for liberty, it stands for the Constitution and the Bill of Rights and those documents are not just words, they are true, well thought-out ideas that as American citizens we all are entitled to.

Chapter 25

One needs to appreciate and be thankful for all of the things that we have in this country. This is the greatest country in the world. At times we may complain about it - and we should be thankful that we have the freedom to complain about it - but no matter how you slice it, America is the best.

The world has a real love/hate relationship with America. There are some countries that have a real hatred of America and what it stands for. It's very true that it's lonely at the top - whether you're a CEO, or in a position of authority or number one at anything, there will always be those who hate you for it - be they individual or country. It's just jealousy.

Of course, misery loves company and there are plenty out there who want Americans to be miserable. Some are religious zealots, theocracies that don't have the freedoms that we have, that feel that the US is a threat to their country's style of government and they hate the US because of it.

There are Muslims in this country who're trying to slowly change or break the laws of the United States. There are incidents in Minnesota of Islamic cabdrivers not picking up American citizens who have a bottle of beer or a bottle of wine in their grocery bags. They won't pick them up because alcohol is not consumed in the Muslim religion.

No one is forcing them to consume any alcohol and it's in a bottle and it's not going to harm them. They don't have to touch it; it won't burn them like the Wicked Witch of the West. The sight of a bottle of alcohol won't cause them to melt down.

But they will melt down our laws, our rights. As a citizen, when I can't hail a cab and go home and bring my groceries along with me because I may have bought some ham, some pork, some beer, some wine - that is ludicrous. We have people suing so that they can wear burkas that hide their identity and they want those pictures to be on their driver's licenses. That too is ludicrous! That is terrorism breaking down our laws. That's what we need to guard against.

It's not just Muslims either, there are other Fundamentalists who want to turn the United States into a Christian theocracy. They want this nation to be a Christian nation, despite the fact that the Constitution protects the right to practice any religion. There are pharmacists who won't fill prescriptions, and creationists who want to erode our science programs.

I've been a good Catholic my entire life, and I feel that if one reads the Bible and understands the lessons, there's no better book to take lessons from. A lot of what's in there is really helpful, but I've never been a religious zealot. In fact I'm quite cautious about those who wear their religion on their sleeves. Even if it's a religion that you believe in, you should always be wary of those who want to destroy all opposition and forbid any discourse.

Whether it be foreign, or domestic, all of the hate is for the wrong reasons. We allow everyone - through freedom of speech - to demean us and say bad things about us. We allow people to come in and if they badmouth the country we don't throw them in jail. We respect the freedoms even of people who don't deserve it.

People should remember that this country has done a lot, and does a lot, for people around the world. But who is doing that? Is it the country or is it the people of this country? This country does not produce any goods nor does it generate any money. It's the people who produce the goods, the people who pay the taxes and it's the American people who make it possible for our government to donate to other governments and to other countries. It is our own relief efforts that help those in need.

The hatred is probably only from a small vocal group, who get played up because they can't get away with the same dissent in their own countries. Ironically, the dislike that we hear about happens because they are free to protest without fear of punishment or incarceration, which is our strongest suit. We're the only country that defends the right for someone to burn the flag. I don't agree with those who do it, but I do agree that they should have the freedom to do so.

Sometimes it can be hard to appreciate things that are so commonplace, that have always just been there and that you've grown up always having. For people like me, however, who lived through a different time and have had the experience of a not having, and of having to work hard to even get the opportunity to have a better life, then that appreciation is multiplied a thousandfold for what this country really is and what it stands for.

There are plenty of Americans who complain that this country could be better. Sure, anything *could* be better, but when you're already the best, you must take care to guard and protect what you have.

What we have is envied by most in the world, but this great Republic of the United States of America didn't just happen, it didn't just come to be by the nature of evolution, but by the wisdom and inspiration of its citizens, guided by their faith, and at a high cost of human life and sacrifice.

Of course there have always been cynics, but I would challenge any one of them who complains about something in this country being wrong to make it better. I'd ask them, "What are you doing to make it better?" If you're going to be cynical about this country, if you're going to complain then you have the responsibility to put out the effort to find a solution to the problem.

The citizens of this country are wonderful, generous people. They may not be perfect in every turn, but they're also not the evildoers that some people would say that they are. We should not use our liberties to undermine the country as some do. We shouldn't go around embracing people like Chavez or Castro and saying that they're good people after knowing what they're doing to their own people. That is wrong, that's not respecting this country. To respect this country, and what it stands for, is to be honest with what's happening.

A lot of the criticism is just jaded cynicism without any true justification, which doesn't really get you anywhere. What good is it to always be negative and be cynical about a country that is doing great things? The real question is, how would you give back to the country?

We give all the time. This country, as I said, is a generous country and it does a lot for the world. And you know, sometimes the United States doesn't get the credit. But that's okay too, because if you give just to get the credit, then you haven't given willingly.

But we give and I believe that it is ultimately appreciated. Sometimes maybe it's not vocalized or verbalized, or told to the others that can't see it, but those who receive it know. Our country gives in many ways, and it's not always the financial aid that is the most important part.

America has been an extraordinary country in the past and is still extraordinary today. I believe that America is the cornerstone of modern civilization. Many early civilizations were great as well, but when you take into account all of the technological evolution and innovation and all of the new things that have been put forth over the centuries, then you'll see as I do, that the United States is the greatest civilization, the greatest country that has ever been in the existence of the world.

All of the strongest civilizations in the world were great because they had discipline, they had respect for the rule of law. They had respect for family. They had respect for government, and education. The citizens respected the laws and their civilizations prospered.

History also shows that when those civilizations got to the point where the order started to break down, where the family unit wasn't cohesive, when the respect for its laws were abandoned, it creates an extremist, anything goes attitude, and those civilizations ended.

If you look at the Greeks, Romans, Egyptians, or any other of the great civilizations of the past, you'll see that when the society started disregarding their laws then their civilization went downhill at a rapid pace and they lost everything.

This country got to the top because of respect that its citizens had for its laws but lately we have a society that feels that accountability doesn't matter. As long as you can blame the other guy, it's their responsibility.

Individual rights don't matter if they are to the detriment of others. People shouldn't be saying that their individual rights supersede everyone else's and that their country is responsible for taking care of them. People shouldn't feel that they simply have no accountability for themselves.

If I burn myself with a cup of coffee, it's not my fault, it's the fault of the one that I bought the cup of coffee from. If I'm drunk and I fall on the sidewalk, it's the fault of the owner of the property that the sidewalk is on, because the sidewalk was hard and I smashed my face in.

We flat out should not have ridiculous things of that nature in the court system. The judiciary supports these frivolous trials, and the attorneys take advantage of whatever abrasiveness is out there among the jurors and they award these ungodly sums of money to people that really don't deserve it.

It all boils down to the fact that the accountability is not there - I mean can you imagine someone breaking into your house then getting hurt while doing so suing you because you didn't have some safety feature in your house. It's ridiculous but it happens.

It's always somebody else's fault. There's no responsibility, no accountability. Accountability. That's the key. No accountability, no law, no rule.

I believe, truly, that United States is the greatest country in the world and I believe that we have to protect it to keep it that way.

I often say that I'm proud to be Italian, but I am more proud to be an American. I'm an Italian by birth, but I'm an American by choice. That means a lot to me. I love my birthplace and my homeland, but I love where I live. I love where I made my home. America is my home.

I recommended that every citizen of this country take the responsibility for their civic duties, because if you don't give anything to your community, then your community isn't going to prosper after a while. Those who think that they have a right to be in this country just because it's here should be reminded that being an American is a privilege - for some it's by birthright, but for those like myself who had to work to earn the right to become a citizen, it's even more so, and I appreciate it all the more.

Honestly, I don't think that any amount of my giving back will ever be able to equal all of the things that I've been given and that God has blessed me and my family with, but I think that's what keeps me going. If I sat and dwelled on any negative situation, then my perspective is negative which just makes things seem worse and worse and worse.

If we dwell on all of the things that we have - and really, just waking up in the morning is something to be thankful for - you start your day out on a positive note, and if you just continue with that positive feeling and bring it to one or two people a day that's giving back. The simplest thing that you can do is to help someone genuinely.

In my life, I've found that simply helping folks is the most rewarding experience that you can have. If there is any way that you can help someone, go ahead and do it. It just comes back - in goodwill, in self gratification. When you help someone, in the long run, it's like a circle. You create a circle of goodwill, and that circle of goodwill is going to come back around to you. So giving back is the easiest thing that any of us can do.

I believe that being in a position to help others is true success. You can achieve all the success in the world and I still have a long way to go before I'd consider myself to be at that level, but I've had a good life, I enjoy my lifestyle. I think it could be better and I always work hard to make it so, but along the way what is truly a heartfelt pleasure, is to know that I've helped somebody else, and that means a lot to me.

Generosity towards others is what makes a person great. It's what makes a country great, and there is no other country on this Earth that is as generous as the United States. Even when we go to war, after we conquer the evil forces, we don't conquer the country, we reestablish them.

Rather, we put them back on their feet and we make those societies better than what they had been before. The United States doesn't take over by power and then usurp those country's resources or the people in any way, shape or form. When called upon to help those in need, the Americans always perform.

Chapter 26

I've had all of these beliefs before I ever set foot on American soil. And again I repeat: that is the reason I loved America before I ever set foot on it. To love this country and to honor this country is really a privilege. It's the best thing I could have hoped for.

I may be here on Earth by the grace of God, and I often say that God has granted me some good things in my life, but I'm not here in America just because of God. I'm here because others worked hard so that I could come to this country, and find the opportunity to become successful.

I've been a business owner for all my adult life and I've enjoyed the fruits of my labor. I'm not saying that I've achieved all things in life, but I'm pleased with what I've been granted to achieve, and I owe most of it to my family.

I have great love for family. That's just the way I was brought up. I've never had any major disagreement with any of my siblings - Anna Igida, Ortensia (God rest her soul), Pasquale, Concetta or Loreta - and to me that is wonderful.

It's a tribute to our wonderful parents, Enrico and Anna Maria. We've always gotten along and we will continue to get along as long as we're alive and we just thank God for being the type of family that always supports one another, and would do anything to help each other succeed.

Those things were instilled in us by our parents. We were always taught to look out for each other and to be appreciative of what we had and what we wanted to have. We've all had our tough times, but we always stuck it through, working together to pull through the hardships.

If I can go from a poor farm boy, working the fields and hauling manure on a donkey, to becoming first a business owner, and then a multi-business owner, then I think that that's quite an achievement. If I can do what I've done and if I can achieve what I've achieved in the United States of America, then there is no one in this country who can't achieve the same. We all have the same opportunity.

Certainly I wasn't born with a silver spoon in my mouth. Instead I had to take it upon myself, along with the support of the people around me, to establish my goals and see them through. My parents supported me all the way, all the time and I'm quite thankful and I'm quite grateful. It means a lot to me that someone like me can come over to this country poor, with only a few clothes and a single pair of shoes and starting from those lowly beginnings, can achieve a good and comfortable life.

My immediate family sacrificed much to make it possible for me to come to America, but it was my father-in-law and mother-in-law, Luigi and Rose Badalamente and my bubbly wife Patti, who continued with the same love and support in making my life fruitful.

One of the happiest days of my life in America was January 9, 1974 when I became a father and Luigi Ferrari was born. The next happiest day of my life was on November 25, 1975 - the birth of my daughter Clarissa. I hope that I have instilled in them the same ideals that my parents taught me, and that they will continue to pass our love and respect of America down through the generations.

While I must admit that it upsets me to hear untrue or unjust statements about America, and it's hard to see disrespect directed towards our law and our flag, I understand clearly that as ugly as dissent can be to a loyal citizen, it is that ability to voice our dissent, along with all our other freedoms, that makes the United States a great country.

Those of us who think that we are helpless to do anything to protect our beliefs, our way of life and our values, need to think again. Outsiders are coming here in devious and illegal ways and using our own laws of freedom against us. I ask you - what will it take you as American citizens to use your right to protest and your right to vote to elect leaders who follow our Constitution?

Most times, whether in business, personal relationships, or in politics, we as Humans have a tendency to let things hit bottom before we react. However, in today's world, with today's adversaries, we absolutely cannot afford to let it bottom out. Our Constitution, and the Declaration it sprung from, with our guarantees of life, liberty and the pursuit of happiness will not survive and we cannot afford to let those who wish harm to the United States succeed.

It begins with the simple realization that we are a nation of laws and if we don't respect those laws we not only disrespect our country, but our very existence. It is the responsibility of each and every one of us to do our utmost to insure our and our country's survival. We must remain vigilant to the detractors and abusers of human rights worldwide.

We should not, and ultimately cannot, forcibly make other countries respect human rights, but we can certainly encourage other countries to respect those rights by our own example. It is our duty as citizens of this country to encourage our fellow Americans to respect not only other beings, but the system and laws that make our civilization possible.

We must challenge ourselves to respect our laws and our Constitution and encourage others to do the same. America is the best country in the world. We have the most freedoms, the most liberty and are the only country in the world founded in part on the principle of the pursuit of happiness. If we don't protect it we will surely lose it.

Never forget that this is your country and that if you don't like what's going on you have the power to change it. Sitting home and complaining to family, friends and neighbors isn't enough. Your Congressmen and your president represent you. By the people, of the people, for the people - it's your government, and you have the power to change things by voting and by staying active in your community.

Freedom, liberty, opportunity, democracy - these are the reasons why I loved America before I ever set foot upon her. These are the reasons why I'm proud to be an American.

APPENDIX I

The Declaration of Independence

My sincere thanks to you the reader. The next 43 pages of this book are the most important pages you will read in your life here on earth.

The Declaration of Independence of the Thirteen Colonies

In CONGRESS, July 4, 1776

The unanimous Declaration of the thirteen united States of America,

When in the Course of human events, it becomes necessary for one people to dissolve the political bands which have connected them with another, and to assume among the powers of the earth, the separate and equal station to which the Laws of Nature and of Nature's God entitle them, a decent respect to the opinions of mankind requires that they should declare the causes which impel them to the separation.

We hold these truths to be self-evident, that all men are created equal, that they are endowed by their Creator with certain unalienable Rights, that among these are Life, Liberty and the pursuit of Happiness. --That to secure these rights, Governments are instituted among Men, deriving their just powers from the consent of the governed, --That whenever any Form of Government becomes destructive of these ends, it is the Right of the People to alter or to abolish it, and to institute new Government, laying its foundation on such principles and organizing its powers in such form, as to them shall seem most likely to effect their Safety and Happiness. Prudence, indeed, will dictate that Governments long established should not be changed for light and transient causes; and accordingly all experience hath shewn, that mankind are more disposed to suffer, while evils are sufferable, than to right themselves by abolishing the forms to which they are accustomed. But when a long train of abuses and usurpations, pursuing invariably the same Object evinces a design to reduce them under absolute Despotism, it is their right, it is their duty, to throw off such Government, and to provide new Guards for their future security. —Such has been the patient sufferance of these Colonies; and such is now the necessity which constrains them to alter their former Systems of Government. The history of the present King of Great Britain [George III] is a history of repeated injuries and usurpations, all having in direct object the establishment of an absolute Tyranny over these States. To prove this, let Facts be submitted to a candid world.

He has refused his Assent to Laws, the most wholesome and necessary for the public good.

He has forbidden his Governors to pass Laws of immediate and pressing importance, unless suspended in their operation till his Assent should be obtained; and when so suspended, he has utterly neglected to attend to them.

He has refused to pass other Laws for the accommodation of large districts of people, unless those people would relinquish the right of Representation in the Legislature, a right inestimable to them and formidable to tyrants only.

He has called together legislative bodies at places unusual, uncomfortable, and distant from the depository of their public Records, for the sole purpose of fatiguing them into compliance with his measures

He has dissolved Representative Houses repeatedly, for opposing with manly firmness his invasions on the rights of the people.

He has refused for a long time, after such dissolutions, to cause others to be elected; whereby the Legislative powers, incapable of Annihilation, have returned to the People at large for their exercise; the State remaining in the mean time exposed to all the dangers of invasion from without, and convulsions within.

He has endeavoured to prevent the population of these States; for that purpose obstructing the Laws for Naturalization of Foreigners; refusing to pass others to encourage their migrations hither, and raising the conditions of new Appropriations of Lands.

He has obstructed the Administration of Justice, by refusing his Assent to Laws for establishing Judiciary powers.

He has made Judges dependent on his Will alone, for the tenure of their offices, and the amount and payment of their salaries.

He has erected a multitude of New Offices, and sent hither swarms of Officers to harass our people, and eat out their substance.

He has kept among us, in times of peace, Standing Armies without the consent of our legislatures.

He has affected to render the Military independent of and superior to the Civil power.

He has combined with others to subject us to a jurisdiction foreign to our constitution and unacknowledged by our laws; giving his Assent to their Acts of pretended Legislation:

For Quartering large bodies of armed troops among us:

For protecting them, by a mock Trial, from punishment for any Murders which they should commit on the Inhabitants of these States:

For cutting off our Trade with all parts of the world:

For imposing Taxes on us without our Consent:

For depriving us, in many cases, of the benefits of Trial by Jury:

For transporting us beyond Seas to be tried for pretended offences:

For abolishing the free System of English Laws in a neighbouring Province, establishing therein an Arbitrary government, and enlarging its Boundaries so as to render it at once an example and fit instrument for introducing the same absolute rule into these Colonies:

For taking away our Charters, abolishing our most valuable Laws, and altering fundamentally the Forms of our Governments:

For suspending our own Legislatures, and declaring themselves invested with power to legislate for us in all cases whatsoever.

He has abdicated Government here, by declaring us out of his Protection and waging War against us.

He has plundered our seas, ravaged our Coasts, burnt our towns, and destroyed the lives of our people.

He is at this time transporting large Armies of foreign Mercenaries to compleat the works of death, desolation and tyranny, already begun with circumstances of Cruelty and perfidy scarcely paralleled in the most barbarous ages, and totally unworthy the Head of a civilized nation.

He has constrained our fellow Citizens taken Captive on the high Seas to bear Arms against their Country, to become the executioners of their friends and Brethren, or to fall themselves by their Hands.

He has excited domestic insurrections amongst us, and has endeavoured to bring on the inhabitants of our frontiers, the merciless Indian Savages, whose known rule of warfare, is an undistinguished destruction of all ages, sexes and conditions.

In every stage of these Oppressions We have Petitioned for Redress in the most humble terms: Our repeated Petitions have been answered only by repeated injury. A Prince whose character is thus marked by every act which may define a Tyrant, is unfit to be the ruler of a free people.

Nor have We been wanting in attentions to our British brethren. We have warned them from time to time of attempts by their legislature to extend an unwarrantable jurisdiction over us. We have reminded them of the circumstances of our emigration and settlement here. We have appealed to their native justice and magnanimity, and we have conjured them by the ties of our common kindred to disavow these usurpations, which, would inevitably interrupt our connections and correspondence. They too have been deaf to the voice of justice and of consanguinity. We must, therefore, acquiesce in the necessity, which denounces our Separation, and hold them, as we hold the rest of mankind, Enemies in War, in Peace Friends.

We, therefore, the Representatives of the united States of America, in General Congress, Assembled, appealing to the Supreme Judge of the world for the rectitude of our intentions, do, in the Name, and by the Authority of the good People of these Colonies, solemnly publish and declare, That these United Colonies are, and of Right ought to be Free and Independent States; that they are Absolved from all Allegiance to the British Crown, and that all political connection between them and the State of Great Britain, is and ought to be totally dissolved; and that as Free and Independent States, they have full Power to levy War, conclude Peace, contract Alliances, establish Commerce, and to do all other Acts and Things which Independent States may of right do. And for the support of this Declaration, with a firm reliance on the protection of divine Providence, we mutually pledge to each other our Lives, our Fortunes and our sacred Honor.

The signers of the Declaration represented the new states as follows:

New Hampshire
Josiah Bartlett, William Whipple, Matthew Thornton

Massachusetts
John Hancock, Samuel Adams, John Adams, Robert Treat Paine, Elbridge Gerry

Rhode Island
Stephen Hopkins, William Ellery

Connecticut
Roger Sherman, Samuel Huntington, William Williams, Oliver Wolcott

New York
William Floyd, Philip Livingston, Francis Lewis, Lewis Morris

New Jersey
Richard Stockton, John Witherspoon, Francis Hopkinson, John Hart, Abraham Clark

Pennsylvania
Robert Morris, Benjamin Rush, Benjamin Franklin, John Morton, George Clymer, James Smith, George Taylor, James Wilson, George Ross

Delaware
Caesar Rodney, George Read, Thomas McKean

Maryland
Samuel Chase, William Paca, Thomas Stone, Charles Carroll of Carrollton

Virginia
George Wythe, Richard Henry Lee, Thomas Jefferson, Benjamin Harrison, Thomas Nelson, Jr., Francis Lightfoot Lee, Carter Braxton

North Carolina
William Hooper, Joseph Hewes, John Penn

South Carolina
Edward Rutledge, Thomas Heyward, Jr., Thomas Lynch, Jr., Arthur Middleton

Georgia
Button Gwinnett, Lyman Hall, George Walton

APPENDIX II

The Constitution of the
United States of America

The Constitution of the United States of America

We the People of the United States, in Order to form a more perfect Union, establish Justice, insure domestic Tranquility, provide for the common defence, promote the general Welfare, and secure the Blessings of Liberty to ourselves and our Posterity, do ordain and establish this Constitution for the United States of America.

Article 1.

Section 1
All legislative Powers herein granted shall be vested in a Congress of the United States, which shall consist of a Senate and House of Representatives.

Section 2
The House of Representatives shall be composed of Members chosen every second Year by the People of the several States, and the Electors in each State shall have the Qualifications requisite for Electors of the most numerous Branch of the State Legislature.

No Person shall be a Representative who shall not have attained to the Age of twenty five Years, and been seven Years a Citizen of the United States, and who shall not, when elected, be an Inhabitant of that State in which he shall be chosen.

Representatives and direct Taxes shall be apportioned among the several States which may be included within this Union, according to their respective Numbers, which shall be determined by adding to the whole Number of free Persons, including those bound to Service for a Term of Years, and excluding Indians not taxed, three fifths of all other Persons.

The actual Enumeration shall be made within three Years after the first Meeting of the Congress of the United States, and within every subsequent Term of ten Years, in such Manner as they shall by Law direct. The Number of Representatives shall not exceed one for every thirty Thousand, but each State shall have at Least one Representative; and until such enumeration shall be made, the State of New Hampshire shall be entitled to choose three, Massachusetts eight, Rhode Island and Providence Plantations one, Connecticut five, New York six, New Jersey four, Pennsylvania eight, Delaware one, Maryland
six, Virginia ten, North Carolina five, South Carolina five and Georgia three.

When vacancies happen in the Representation from any State, the Executive Authority thereof shall issue Writs of Election to fill such Vacancies.

The House of Representatives shall choose their Speaker and other Officers; and shall have the sole Power of Impeachment.

Section 3
The Senate of the United States shall be composed of two Senators from each State, chosen by the Legislature thereof, for six Years; and each Senator shall have one Vote.

Immediately after they shall be assembled in Consequence of the first Election, they shall be divided as equally as may be into three Classes. The Seats of the Senators of the first Class shall be vacated at the Expiration of the second Year, of the second Class at the Expiration of the fourth Year, and of the third Class at the Expiration of the sixth Year, so that one third may be chosen every second Year; and if Vacancies happen by Resignation, or otherwise, during the Recess of the Legislature of any State, the Executive thereof may make temporary Appointments until the next Meeting of the Legislature, which shall then fill such Vacancies.

No person shall be a Senator who shall not have attained to the Age of thirty Years, and been nine Years a Citizen of the United States, and who shall not, when elected, be an Inhabitant of that State for which he shall be chosen.

The Vice President of the United States shall be President of the Senate, but shall have no Vote, unless they be equally divided.

The Senate shall choose their other Officers, and also a President pro tempore, in the absence of the Vice President, or when he shall exercise the Office of President of the United States.

The Senate shall have the sole Power to try all Impeachments. When sitting for that Purpose, they shall be on Oath or Affirmation. When the President of the United States is tied, the Chief Justice shall preside: And no Person shall be convicted without the Concurrence of two thirds of the Members present.

Judgment in Cases of Impeachment shall not extend further than to removal from Office, and disqualification to hold and enjoy any Office of honor, Trust or Profit under the United States: but the Party convicted shall nevertheless be liable and subject to Indictment, Trial, Judgment and Punishment, according to Law.

Section 4
The Times, Places and Manner of holding Elections for Senators and Representatives, shall be prescribed in each State by the Legislature thereof; but the Congress may at any time

by Law make or alter such Regulations, except as to the Place of Choosing Senators.

The Congress shall assemble at least once in every Year, and such Meeting shall be on the first Monday in December, unless they shall by Law appoint a different Day.

Section 5
Each House shall be the Judge of the Elections, Returns and Qualifications of its own Members, and a Majority of each shall constitute a Quorum to do Business; but a smaller number may adjourn from day to day, and may be authorized to compel the Attendance of absent Members, in such Manner, and under such Penalties as each House may provide.

Each House may determine the Rules of its Proceedings, punish its Members for disorderly Behavior, and, with the Concurrence of two-thirds, expel a Member.

Each House shall keep a Journal of its Proceedings, and from time to time publish the same, excepting such Parts as may in their Judgment require Secrecy; and the Yeas and Nays of the Members of either House on any question shall, at the Desire of one fifth of those Present, be entered on the Journal.

Neither House, during the Session of Congress, shall, without the Consent of the other, adjourn for more than three days, nor to any other Place than that in which the two Houses shall be sitting.

Section 6
The Senators and Representatives shall receive a Compensation for their Services, to be ascertained by Law, and paid out of the Treasury of the United States. They shall in all Cases, except Treason, Felony and Breach of the Peace, be privileged

from Arrest during their Attendance at the Session of their respective Houses, and in going to and returning from the same; and for any Speech or Debate in either House, they shall not be questioned in any other Place.

No Senator or Representative shall, during the Time for which he was elected, be appointed to any civil Office under the Authority of the United States which shall have been created, or the Emoluments whereof shall have been increased during such time; and no Person holding any Office under the United States, shall be a Member of either House during his Continuance in Office.

Section 7

All bills for raising Revenue shall originate in the House of Representatives; but the Senate may propose or concur with Amendments as on other Bills.

Every Bill which shall have passed the House of Representatives and the Senate, shall, before it become a Law, be presented to the President of the United States; If he approve he shall sign it, but if not he shall return it, with his
Objections to that House in which it shall have originated, who shall enter the Objections at large on their Journal, and proceed to reconsider it. If after such Reconsideration two thirds of that House shall agree to pass the Bill, it shall be sent, together with the Objections, to the other House, by which it shall likewise be reconsidered, and if approved by two thirds of that House, it shall become a Law. But in all such Cases the Votes of both Houses shall be determined by Yeas and Nays, and the Names of the Persons voting for and against the Bill shall be entered on the Journal of each House respectively. If any Bill shall not be returned by the President within ten Days (Sundays excepted) after it shall have been presented to him, the Same shall be a Law, in like Manner as if he had signed it,

unless the Congress by their Adjournment prevent its Return, in which Case it shall not be a Law.

Every Order, Resolution, or Vote to which the Concurrence of the Senate and House of Representatives may be necessary (except on a question of Adjournment) shall be presented to the President of the United States; and before the Same shall take Effect, shall be approved by him, or being disapproved by him, shall be repassed by two thirds of the Senate and House of Representatives, according to the Rules and Limitations prescribed in the Case of a Bill.

Section 8
The Congress shall have Power To lay and collect Taxes, Duties, Imposts and Excises, to pay the Debts and provide for the common Defence and general Welfare of the United States; but all Duties, Imposts and Excises shall be uniform throughout the United States;

To borrow money on the credit of the United States;

To regulate Commerce with foreign Nations, and among the several States, and with the Indian Tribes;

To establish an uniform Rule of Naturalization, and uniform Laws on the subject of Bankruptcies throughout the United States;

To coin Money, regulate the Value thereof, and of foreign Coin, and fix the Standard of Weights and Measures;

To provide for the Punishment of counterfeiting the Securities and current Coin of the United States;

To establish Post Offices and Post Roads;

To promote the Progress of Science and useful Arts, by securing for limited Times to Authors and Inventors the exclusive Right to their respective Writings and Discoveries;

To constitute Tribunals inferior to the supreme Court;

To define and punish Piracies and Felonies committed on the high Seas, and Offenses against the Law of Nations;

To declare War, grant Letters of Marque and Reprisal, and make Rules concerning Captures on Land and Water;

To raise and support Armies, but no Appropriation of Money to that Use shall be for a longer Term than two Years;

To provide and maintain a Navy;

To make Rules for the Government and Regulation of the land and naval Forces;

To provide for calling forth the Militia to execute the Laws of the Union, suppress Insurrections and repel Invasions;

To provide for organizing, arming, and disciplining the Militia, and for governing such Part of them as may be employed in the Service of the United States, reserving to the States respectively, the Appointment of the Officers, and the Authority of training the Militia according to the discipline prescribed by Congress;

To exercise exclusive Legislation in all Cases whatsoever, over such District (not exceeding ten Miles square) as may, by Cession of particular States, and the acceptance of Congress, become the Seat of the Government of the United States, and to exercise like Authority over all Places purchased by the Consent of the Legislature of the State in which the Same shall be, for the Erection of Forts, Magazines, Arsenals, dock-Yards, and other needful Buildings; And

To make all Laws which shall be necessary and proper for carrying into Execution the foregoing Powers, and all other Powers vested by this Constitution in the Government of the United States, or in any Department or Officer thereof.

Section 9

The Migration or Importation of such Persons as any of the States now existing shall think proper to admit, shall not be prohibited by the Congress prior to the Year one thousand eight hundred and eight, but a tax or duty may be imposed on such Importation, not exceeding ten dollars for each Person.

The privilege of the Writ of Habeas Corpus shall not be suspended, unless when in Cases of Rebellion or Invasion the public Safety may require it.

No Bill of Attainder or ex post facto Law shall be passed.

No capitation, or other direct, Tax shall be laid, unless in Proportion to the Census or Enumeration herein before directed to be taken.

No Tax or Duty shall be laid on Articles exported from any State.

No Preference shall be given by any Regulation of Commerce or Revenue to the Ports of one State over those of another: nor shall Vessels bound to, or from, one State, be obliged to enter, clear, or pay Duties in another.

No Money shall be drawn from the Treasury, but in Consequence of Appropriations made by Law; and a regular Statement and Account of the Receipts and Expenditures of all public Money shall be published from time to time.

No Title of Nobility shall be granted by the United States: And no Person holding any Office of Profit or Trust under them, shall, without the Consent of the Congress, accept of any present, Emolument, Office, or Title, of any kind whatever, from any King, Prince or foreign State.

Section 10

No State shall enter into any Treaty, Alliance, or Confederation; grant Letters of Marque and Reprisal; coin Money; emit Bills of Credit; make any Thing but gold and silver Coin a Tender in Payment of Debts; pass any Bill of Attainder, ex post facto Law, or Law impairing the Obligation of Contracts, or grant any Title of Nobility.

No State shall, without the Consent of the Congress, lay any Imposts or Duties on Imports or Exports, except what may be absolutely necessary for executing its inspection Laws: and the net Produce of all Duties and Imposts, laid by any State on Imports or Exports, shall be for the Use of the Treasury of the United States; and all such Laws shall be subject to the Revision and Control of the Congress.

No State shall, without the Consent of Congress, lay any duty of Tonnage, keep Troops, or Ships of War in time of Peace, enter into any Agreement or Compact with another State, or with a foreign Power, or engage in War, unless actually invaded, or in such imminent Danger as will not admit of delay.

Article 2.

<u>Section 1</u>
The executive Power shall be vested in a President of the United States of America. He shall hold his Office during the Term of four Years, and, together with the Vice-President chosen for the same Term, be elected, as follows:

Each State shall appoint, in such Manner as the Legislature thereof may direct, a Number of Electors, equal to the whole Number of Senators and Representatives to which the State may be entitled in the Congress: but no Senator or Representative, or Person holding an Office of Trust or Profit under the United States, shall be appointed an Elector.

The Electors shall meet in their respective States, and vote by Ballot for two persons, of whom one at least shall not lie an Inhabitant of the same State with themselves. And they shall make a List of all the Persons voted for, and of the Number of Votes for each; which List they shall sign and certify, and transmit sealed to the Seat of the Government of the United States, directed to the President of the Senate. The President of the Senate shall, in the Presence of the Senate and House of Representatives, open all the Certificates, and the Votes shall then be counted. The Person having the greatest Number of Votes shall be the President, if such Number be a Majority of the whole Number of Electors appointed; and if there be more than one who have such Majority, and have an equal Number of Votes, then the House of Representatives shall immediately choose by Ballot one of them for President; and if no Person have a Majority, then from the five highest on the List the said House shall in like Manner choose the President. But in choosing the President, the Votes shall betaken by States, the Representation from each State having one Vote; a quorum for this Purpose shall consist of a Member or Members from two-thirds of the States, and a Majority of all the States shall be necessary to a Choice. In every Case, after the Choice of the President, the Person having the greatest Number of Votes of the Electors shall be the Vice President. But if there should remain two or more who have equal Votes, the Senate shall choose from them by Ballot the Vice-President.

The Congress may determine the Time of choosing the Electors, and the Day on which they shall give their Votes; which Day shall be the same throughout the United States.

No person except a natural born Citizen, or a Citizen of the United States, at the time of the Adoption of this Constitution, shall be eligible to the Office of President; neither shall any Person be eligible to that Office who shall not have attained to the Age of thirty-five Years, and been fourteen Years a Resident within the United States.

In Case of the Removal of the President from Office, or of his Death, Resignation, or Inability to discharge the Powers and Duties of the said Office, the same shall devolve on the Vice President, and the Congress may by Law provide for the Case of Removal, Death, Resignation or Inability, both of the President and Vice President, declaring what Officer shall then act as President, and such Officer shall act accordingly, until the Disability be removed, or a President shall be elected.

The President shall, at stated Times, receive for his Services, a Compensation, which shall neither be increased nor diminished during the Period for which he shall have been elected, and he shall not receive within that Period any other Emolument from the United States, or any of them.

Before he enter on the Execution of his Office, he shall take the following Oath or Affirmation:

"I do solemnly swear (or affirm) that I will faithfully execute the Office of President of the United States, and will to the best of my Ability, preserve, protect and defend the Constitution of the United States."

Section 2
The President shall be Commander in Chief of the Army and Navy of the United States, and of the Militia of the several States, when called into the actual Service of the United States; he may require the Opinion, in writing, of the principal Officer in each of the executive Departments, upon any subject relating to the Duties of their respective Offices, and he shall have Power to Grant Reprieves and Pardons for Offenses against the United States, except in Cases of Impeachment.

He shall have Power, by and with the Advice and Consent of the Senate, to make Treaties, provided two thirds of the Senators present concur; and he shall nominate, and by and with the Advice and Consent of the Senate, shall appoint Ambassadors, other public Ministers and Consuls, Judges of the supreme Court, and all other Officers of the United States, whose Appointments are not herein otherwise provided for, and which shall be established by Law: but the Congress may by Law vest the Appointment of such inferior Officers, as they think proper, in the President alone, in the Courts of Law, or in the Heads of Departments.

The President shall have Power to fill up all Vacancies that may happen during the Recess of the Senate, by granting Commissions which shall expire at the End of their next Session.

Section 3

He shall from time to time give to the Congress Information of the State of the Union, and recommend to their Consideration such Measures as he shall judge necessary and expedient; he may, on extraordinary Occasions, convene both Houses, or either of them, and in Case of Disagreement between them, with Respect to the Time of Adjournment, he may adjourn them to such Time as he shall think proper; he shall receive Ambassadors and other public Ministers; he shall take Care that the Laws be faithfully executed, and shall Commission all the Officers of the United States.

Section 4

The President, Vice President and all civil Officers of the United States, shall be removed from Office on Impeachment for, and Conviction of, Treason, Bribery, or other high Crimes and Misdemeanors.

Article 3.

Section 1

The judicial Power of the United States, shall be vested in one supreme Court, and in such inferior Courts as the Congress may from time to time ordain and establish. The Judges, both of the supreme and inferior Courts, shall hold their Offices during good Behavior, and shall, at stated Times, receive for their Services a Compensation which shall not be diminished during their Continuance in Office.

Section 2

The judicial Power shall extend to all Cases, in Law and Equity, arising under this Constitution, the Laws of the United States, and Treaties made, or which shall be made, under their Authority; to all Cases affecting Ambassadors, other

public Ministers and Consuls; to all Cases of admiralty and maritime
Jurisdiction; to Controversies to which the United States shall be a Party; to Controversies between two or more States; between a State and Citizens of another State; between Citizens of different States; between Citizens of the same State claiming Lands under Grants of different States, and between a State, or the Citizens thereof, and foreign States, Citizens or Subjects.

In all Cases affecting Ambassadors, other public Ministers and Consuls, and those in which a State shall be Party, the supreme Court shall have original Jurisdiction. In all the other Cases before mentioned, the supreme Court shall have appellate Jurisdiction, both as to Law and Fact, with such Exceptions, and under such Regulations as the Congress shall make.

The Trial of all Crimes, except in Cases of Impeachment, shall be by Jury; and such Trial shall be held in the State where the said Crimes shall have been committed; but when not committed within any State, the Trial shall be at such Place or Places as the Congress may by Law have directed.

Section 3
Treason against the United States, shall consist only in levying War against them, or in adhering to their Enemies, giving them Aid and Comfort. No Person shall be convicted of Treason unless on the Testimony of two Witnesses to the same overt Act, or on Confession in open Court.

The Congress shall have power to declare the Punishment of Treason, but no Attainder of Treason shall work Corruption of Blood, or Forfeiture except during the Life of the Person attainted.

Article 4.

Section 1
Full Faith and Credit shall be given in each State to the public Acts, Records, and judicial Proceedings of every other State. And the Congress may by general Laws prescribe the Manner in which such Acts, Records and Proceedings shall be proved, and the Effect thereof.

Section 2
The Citizens of each State shall be entitled to all Privileges and Immunities of Citizens in the several States.

A Person charged in any State with Treason, Felony, or other Crime, who shall flee from Justice, and be found in another State, shall on demand of the executive Authority of the State from which he fled, be delivered up, to be removed to the State having Jurisdiction of the Crime.

No Person held to Service or Labour in one State, under the Laws thereof, escaping into another, shall, in Consequence of any Law or Regulation therein, be discharged from such Service or Labour, But shall be delivered up on Claim of the Party to whom such Service or Labour may be due.

Section 3
New States may be admitted by the Congress into this Union; but no new States shall be formed or erected within the Jurisdiction of any other State; nor any State be formed by the Junction of two or more States, or parts of States, without the Consent of the Legislatures of the States concerned as well as of the Congress.

The Congress shall have Power to dispose of and make all needful Rules and Regulations respecting the Territory or other Property belonging to the United States; and nothing in this Constitution shall be so construed as to Prejudice any Claims of the United States, or of any particular State.

Section 4
The United States shall guarantee to every State in this Union a Republican Form of Government, and shall protect each of them against Invasion; and on Application of the Legislature, or of the Executive (when the Legislature cannot be convened) against domestic Violence.

Article 5.

The Congress, whenever two thirds of both Houses shall deem it necessary, shall propose Amendments to this Constitution, or, on the Application of the Legislatures of two thirds of the several States, shall call a Convention for proposing Amendments, which, in either Case, shall be valid to all Intents and Purposes, as part of this Constitution, when ratified by the Legislatures of three fourths of the several States, or by Conventions in three fourths thereof, as the one or the other Mode of Ratification may be proposed by the Congress; Provided that no Amendment which may be made prior to the Year One thousand eight hundred and eight shall in any Manner affect the first and fourth Clauses in the Ninth Section of the first Article; and that no State, without its Consent, shall be deprived of its equal Suffrage in the Senate.

Article 6.

All Debts contracted and Engagements entered into, before the Adoption of this Constitution, shall be as valid against the United States under this Constitution, as under the Confederation.

This Constitution, and the Laws of the United States which shall be made in Pursuance thereof; and all Treaties made, or which shall be made, under the Authority of the United States, shall be the supreme Law of the Land; and the Judges in every State shall be bound thereby, any Thing in the Constitution or Laws of any State to the Contrary notwithstanding.

The Senators and Representatives before mentioned, and the Members of the several State Legislatures, and all executive and judicial Officers, both of the United States and of the several States, shall be bound by Oath or Affirmation, to support this Constitution; but no religious Test shall ever be required as a Qualification to any Office or public Trust under the United States.

Article 7.

The Ratification of the Conventions of nine States, shall be sufficient for the Establishment of this Constitution between the States so ratifying the Same.

Done in Convention by the Unanimous Consent of the States present the Seventeenth Day of September in the Year of our Lord one thousand seven hundred and Eighty seven and of the Independence of the United States of America the Twelfth. In Witness whereof We have hereunto subscribed our Names.

George Washington - President and deputy from Virginia

New Hampshire - John Langdon, Nicholas Gilman

Massachusetts - Nathaniel Gorham, Rufus King

Connecticut - William Samuel Johnson, Roger Sherman

New York - Alexander Hamilton

New Jersey - William Livingston, David Brearley, William Paterson, Jonathan Dayton

Pennsylvania - Benjamin Franklin, Thomas Mifflin, Robert Morris, George Clymer, Thomas Fitzsimons, Jared Ingersoll, James Wilson, Gouvernour Morris

Delaware - George Read, Gunning Bedford Jr., John Dickinson, Richard Bassett, Jacob Broom

Maryland - James McHenry, Daniel of St Thomas Jenifer, Daniel Carroll

Virginia - John Blair, James Madison Jr.

North Carolina - William Blount, Richard Dobbs Spaight, Hugh Williamson

South Carolina - John Rutledge, Charles Cotesworth Pinckney, Charles Pinckney, Pierce Butler

Georgia - William Few, Abraham Baldwin

Attest: William Jackson, Secretary

The Bill of Rights

December 15, 1791

Amendment 1

Congress shall make no law respecting an establishment of religion, or prohibiting the free exercise thereof; or abridging the freedom of speech, or of the press; or the right of the people peaceably to assemble, and to petition the Government for a redress of grievances.

Amendment 2

A well regulated Militia, being necessary to the security of a free State, the right of the people to keep and bear Arms, shall not be infringed.

Amendment 3

No Soldier shall, in time of peace be quartered in any house, without the consent of the Owner, nor in time of war, but in a manner to be prescribed by law.

Amendment 4

The right of the people to be secure in their persons, houses, papers, and effects, against unreasonable searches and seizures, shall not be violated, and no Warrants shall issue, but upon probable cause, supported by Oath or affirmation, and particularly describing the place to be searched, and the persons or things to be seized.

Amendment 5

No person shall be held to answer for a capital, or otherwise infamous crime, unless on a presentment or indictment of a Grand Jury, except in cases arising in the land or naval forces, or in the Militia, when in actual service in time of War or public danger; nor shall any person be subject for the same offense to be twice put in jeopardy of life or limb; nor shall be compelled in any criminal case to be a witness against himself, nor be deprived of life, liberty, or property, without due process of law; nor shall private property be taken for public use, without just compensation.

Amendment 6

In all criminal prosecutions, the accused shall enjoy the right to a speedy and public trial, by an impartial jury of the State and district wherein the crime shall have been committed, which district shall have been previously ascertained by law, and to be informed of the nature and cause of the accusation; to be confronted with the witnesses against him; to have compulsory process for obtaining witnesses in his favor, and to have the Assistance of Counsel for his defence.

Amendment 7

In Suits at common law, where the value in controversy shall exceed twenty dollars, the right of trial by jury shall be preserved, and no fact tried by a jury, shall be otherwise re-examined in any Court of the United States, than according to the rules of the common law.

Amendment 8

Excessive bail shall not be required, nor excessive fines imposed, nor cruel and unusual punishments inflicted.

Amendment 9

The enumeration in the Constitution, of certain rights, shall not be construed to deny or disparage others retained by the people.

Amendment 10

The powers not delegated to the United States by the Constitution, nor prohibited by it to the States, are reserved to the States respectively, or to the people.

Amendment 11 (February 7, 1795)

The Judicial power of the United States shall not be construed to extend to any suit in law or equity, commenced or prosecuted against one of the United States by Citizens of another State, or by Citizens or Subjects of any Foreign State.

Amendment 12 (June 15, 1804)

The Electors shall meet in their respective states, and vote by ballot for President and Vice-President, one of whom, at least, shall not be an inhabitant of the same state with themselves; they shall name in their ballots the person voted for as President, and in distinct ballots the person voted for as Vice-President, and they shall make distinct lists of all persons voted for as President, and of all persons voted for as Vice-President and of the number of votes for each, which lists they shall sign and certify, and transmit sealed to the seat of the government of the United States, directed to the President of the Senate;

The President of the Senate shall, in the presence of the Senate and House of Representatives, open all the certificates and the votes shall then be counted;

The person having the greatest Number of votes for President, shall be the President, if such number be a majority of the whole number of Electors appointed; and if no person have such majority, then from the persons having the highest numbers not exceeding three on the list of those voted for as President, the House of

Representatives shall choose immediately, by ballot, the President. But in choosing the President, the votes shall be taken by states, the representation from each state having one vote; a quorum for this purpose shall consist of a member or members from two-thirds of the states, and a majority of all the states shall be necessary to a choice. And if the House of Representatives shall not choose a President whenever the right of choice shall devolve upon them, before the fourth day of March next following, then the Vice-President shall act as President, as in the case of the death or other constitutional disability of the President.

The person having the greatest number of votes as Vice-President, shall be the Vice-President, if such number be a majority of the whole number of Electors appointed, and if no person have a majority, then from the two highest numbers on the list, the Senate shall choose the Vice-President; a quorum for the purpose shall consist of two-thirds of the whole number of Senators, and a majority of the whole number shall be necessary to a choice. But no person constitutionally ineligible to the office of President shall be eligible to that of Vice-President of the United States.

Amendment 13 (December 6, 1865)

Section 1
Neither slavery nor involuntary servitude, except as a punishment for crime whereof the party shall have been duly convicted, shall exist within the United States, or any place subject to their jurisdiction.

Section 2
Congress shall have power to enforce this article by appropriate legislation.

Amendment 14 (July 9, 1868)

Section 1
All persons born or naturalized in the United States, and subject to the jurisdiction thereof, are citizens of the United States and of the State wherein they reside. No State shall make or enforce any law which shall abridge the privileges or immunities of citizens of the United States; nor shall any State deprive any person of life, liberty, or property, without due process of law; nor deny to any person within its jurisdiction the equal protection of the laws.

Section 2
Representatives shall be apportioned among the several States according to their respective numbers, counting the whole number of persons in each State, excluding Indians not taxed. But when the right to vote at any election for the choice of electors for President and Vice-President of the United States, Representatives in Congress, the Executive and Judicial officers of a State, or the members of the Legislature thereof, is denied to any of the male inhabitants of such State, being twenty-one years of age, and citizens of the United States, or in any way abridged, except for participation in rebellion, or other crime, the basis of representation therein shall be reduced in the proportion which the number of such male citizens shall

bear to the whole number of male citizens twenty-one years of age in such State.

Section 3

No person shall be a Senator or Representative in Congress, or elector of President and Vice-President, or hold any office, civil or military, under the United States, or under any State, who, having previously taken an oath, as a member of Congress, or as an officer of the United States, or as a member of any State legislature, or as an executive or judicial officer of any State, to support the Constitution of the United States, shall have engaged in insurrection or rebellion against the same, or given aid or comfort to the enemies thereof. But Congress may by a vote of two-thirds of each House, remove such disability.

Section 4

The validity of the public debt of the United States, authorized by law, including debts incurred for payment of pensions and bounties for services in suppressing insurrection or rebellion, shall not be questioned. But neither the United States nor any State shall assume or pay any debt or obligation incurred in aid of insurrection or rebellion against the United States, or any claim for the loss or emancipation of any slave; but all such debts, obligations and claims shall be held illegal and void.

Section 5

The Congress shall have power to enforce, by appropriate legislation, the provisions of this article.

Amendment 15 (February 3, 1870)

Section 1

The right of citizens of the United States to vote shall not be denied or abridged by the United States or by any

State on account of race, color, or previous condition of servitude.

Section 2

The Congress shall have power to enforce this article by appropriate legislation.

Amendment 16 (February 3, 1913)

The Congress shall have power to lay and collect taxes on incomes, from whatever source derived, without apportionment among the several States, and without regard to any census or enumeration.

Amendment 17 (April 8, 1913)

The Senate of the United States shall be composed of two Senators from each State, elected by the people thereof, for six years; and each Senator shall have one vote. The electors in each State shall have the qualifications requisite for electors of the most numerous branch of the State legislatures.

When vacancies happen in the representation of any State in the Senate, the executive authority of such State shall issue writs of election to fill such vacancies: Provided, That the legislature of any State may empower the executive thereof to make temporary appointments until the people fill the vacancies by election as the legislature may direct.

This amendment shall not be so construed as to affect the election or term of any Senator chosen before it becomes valid as part of the Constitution.

Amendment 18 (January 16, 1919)
NOTE: Repealed by the 21st Amendment

Section 1
After one year from the ratification of this article the manufacture, sale, or transportation of intoxicating liquors within, the importation thereof into, or the exportation thereof from the United States and all territory subject to the jurisdiction thereof for beverage purposes is hereby prohibited.

Section 2
The Congress and the several States shall have concurrent power to enforce this article by appropriate legislation.

Section 3
This article shall be inoperative unless it shall have been ratified as an amendment to the Constitution by the legislatures of the several States, as provided in the Constitution, within seven years from the date of the submission hereof to the States by the Congress.

Amendment 19 (August 18, 1920)

The right of citizens of the United States to vote shall not be denied or abridged by the United States or by any State on account of sex.

Congress shall have power to enforce this article by appropriate legislation.

Amendment 20 (January 23, 1933)

Section 1
The terms of the President and Vice President shall end at noon on the 20th day of January, and the terms of Senators and Representatives at noon on the 3d day of January, of the years in which such terms would have ended if this article had not been ratified; and the terms of their successors shall then begin.

Section 2
The Congress shall assemble at least once in every year, and such meeting shall begin at noon on the 3d day of January, unless they shall by law appoint a different day.

Section 3
If, at the time fixed for the beginning of the term of the President, the President elect shall have died, the Vice President elect shall become President. If a President shall not have been chosen before the time fixed for the beginning of his term, or if the President elect shall have failed to qualify, then the Vice President elect shall act as President until a President shall have qualified; and the Congress may by law provide for the case wherein neither a President elect nor a Vice President elect shall have qualified, declaring who shall then act as President, or the manner in which one who is to act shall be selected, and such person shall act accordingly until a President or Vice President shall have qualified.

Section 4
The Congress may by law provide for the case of the death of any of the persons from whom the House of Representatives may choose a President whenever the right of choice shall have devolved upon them, and for the case of the death of any of the persons from whom the Senate may choose a Vice President whenever the right of choice shall have devolved upon them.

Section 5
Sections 1 and 2 shall take effect on the 15th day of October following the ratification of this article.

Section 6
This article shall be inoperative unless it shall have been ratified as an amendment to the Constitution by the legislatures of three-fourths of the several States within seven years from the date of its submission.

Amendment 21 (December 5, 1933)

Section 1
The eighteenth article of amendment to the Constitution of the United States is hereby repealed.

Section 2
The transportation or importation into any State, Territory, or possession of the United States for delivery or use therein of intoxicating liquors, in violation of the laws thereof, is hereby prohibited.

Section 3

The article shall be inoperative unless it shall have been ratified as an amendment to the Constitution by conventions in the several States, as provided in the Constitution, within seven years from the date of the submission hereof to the States by the Congress.

Amendment 22 (February 27, 1951)

Section 1

No person shall be elected to the office of the President more than twice, and no person who has held the office of President, or acted as President, for more than two years of a term to which some other person was elected President shall be elected to the office of the President more than once. But this Article shall not apply to any person holding the office of President, when this Article was proposed by the Congress, and shall not prevent any person who may be holding the office of President, or acting as President, during the term within which this Article becomes operative from holding the office of President or acting as President during the remainder of such term.

Section 2

This article shall be inoperative unless it shall have been ratified as an amendment to the Constitution by the legislatures of three-fourths of the several States within seven years from the date of its submission to the States by the Congress.

Amendment 23 (March 29, 1961)

<u>Section 1</u>
The District constituting the seat of Government of the United States shall appoint in such manner as the Congress may direct: A number of electors of President and Vice President equal to the whole number of Senators and Representatives in Congress to which the District would be entitled if it were a State, but in no event more than the least populous State; they shall be in addition to those appointed by the States, but they shall be considered, for the purposes of the election of President and Vice President, to be electors appointed by a State; and they shall meet in the District and perform such duties as provided by the twelfth article of amendment.

<u>Section 2</u>
The Congress shall have power to enforce this article by appropriate legislation.

Amendment 24 (January 23, 1964)

<u>Section 1</u>
The right of citizens of the United States to vote in any primary or other election for President or Vice President, for electors for President or Vice President, or for Senator or Representative in Congress, shall not be denied or abridged by the United States or any State by reason of failure to pay any poll tax or other tax.

<u>Section 2</u>
The Congress shall have power to enforce this article by appropriate legislation.

Amendment 25 (February 10, 1967)

Section 1
In case of the removal of the President from office or of his death or resignation, the Vice President shall become President.

Section 2
Whenever there is a vacancy in the office of the Vice President, the President shall nominate a Vice President who shall take office upon confirmation by a majority vote of both Houses of Congress.

Section 3
Whenever the President transmits to the President pro tempore of the Senate and the Speaker of the House of Representatives his written declaration that he is unable to discharge the powers and duties of his office, and until he transmits to them a written declaration to the contrary, such powers and duties shall be discharged by the Vice President as Acting President.

Section 4
Whenever the Vice President and a majority of either the principal officers of the executive departments or of such other body as Congress may by law provide, transmit to the President pro tempore of the Senate and the Speaker of the House of Representatives their written declaration that the President is unable to discharge the powers and duties of his office, the Vice President shall immediately

assume the powers and duties of the office as Acting President.

Thereafter, when the President transmits to the President pro tempore of the Senate and the Speaker of the House of Representatives his written declaration that no inability exists, he shall resume the powers and duties of his office unless the Vice President and a majority of either the principal officers of the executive department or of such other body as Congress may by law provide, transmit within four days to the President pro tempore of the Senate and the Speaker of the House of Representatives their written declaration that the President is unable to discharge the powers and duties of his office. Thereupon Congress shall decide the issue, assembling within forty eight hours for that purpose if not in session. If the Congress, within twenty one days after receipt of the latter written declaration, or, if Congress is not in session, within twenty one days after Congress is required to assemble, determines by two thirds vote of both Houses that the President is unable to discharge the powers and duties of his office, the Vice President shall continue to discharge the same as Acting President; otherwise, the President shall resume the powers and duties of his office.

Amendment 26 (July 1, 1971)

Section 1
The right of citizens of the United States, who are eighteen years of age or older, to vote shall not be denied or abridged by the United States or by any State on account of age.

Section 2

The Congress shall have power to enforce this article by appropriate legislation.

Amendment 27 (May 7, 1992)

NOTE: This Amendment was submitted as part of the Bill of Rights on September 25, 1789

No law, varying the compensation for the services of the Senators and Representatives, shall take effect, until an election of Representatives shall have intervened.

About the Author

Franco Ferrari was born in a small town in Italy and became an American by choice and by the grace of God. He received his associate's degree in Business Administration in 1967 and also served 2 years in the U.S. Army during the Vietnam era. Mr. Ferrari was elected President of the cement contractor association at the age of 24 where he became an expert at the art of negotiating contracts. He was a licensed general contractor in Michigan and became a licensed home builder in Florida in 1973. After that venture in 1975 he started a chain of restaurants with family members and grew it to 15 locations before embarking in a business brokerage career in 1985. One of his best decisions was to become the first Sunbelt Business Broker Franchisee in Florida in 1993. Franco was president of the Florida Business Brokers Association Central Florida chapter for two years and served on the state Board of Directors for 10 years. He received the CFBI (Certified Florida Business Intermediary) and was also FBBA training and orientation director for 8 years and was presented the honorary lifetime member award from FBBA as well. In 1997, Mr. Ferrari joined the Institute of Certified Business Counselors and by March

2, 1998 was awarded the Professional Designation of Certified Business Counselor – BCB. Mr. Ferrari also joined IBBA in 1998 and earned the CBI designation in 2004. Franco is a member of SCORE and besides counseling does a monthly seminar on how to start your business. He serves on the advisory boards of both Bank First Community Bank and the Disney-SBA National Entrepreneur Center in Orlando, FL. Franco is also chairman of the program committee at the NEC where he continuously promotes business growth through programs such as: "How to Sell a Business", "How to Buy a Business", and "Exit Strategy & Retirement Planning". Franco serves as chairman on the President's Advisory Counsel of Sunbelt Business Brokers Franchise and always promotes the growth of Central Florida's business community on his weekly radio show "The Business Advisor" giving expert advice on "How to Buy, Grow, and Sell a Business Right!"

I truly loved America before I came here. I now consider myself to be living in Paradise. I have a loving wife and two wonderful children, a daughter-in-law and a son-in-law. We're all living in the tourist capital of the world - Orlando, Florida.

www.ingramcontent.com/pod-product-compliance
Lightning Source LLC
Chambersburg PA
CBHW060616290526
45793CB00001B/51